Third Eye

Awakening

An Essential Guide to Opening Your Third Eye Awakening

(A Guided Meditation Manual to Expand Mind Power)

James McFarland

Published By **Oliver Leish**

James McFarland

Third Eye Awakening: An Essential Guide to Opening Your Third Eye Awakening(A Guided Meditation Manual to Expand Mind Power)

ISBN   978-1-998927-21-0

No part of this guidebook shall be reproduced in any form without permission in writing from the publisher except in the case of brief quotations embodied in critical articles or reviews.

Legal & Disclaimer

The information contained in this book is not designed to replace or take the place of any form of medicine or professional medical advice. The information in this book has been provided for educational & entertainment purposes only.

The information contained in this book has been compiled from sources deemed reliable, and it is accurate to the best of the Author's knowledge; however, the Author cannot guarantee its accuracy and validity and cannot be held liable for any errors or omissions. Changes are periodically made to this book. You must consult your doctor or get professional medical advice before using any of the suggested remedies, techniques, or information in this book.

Table Of Contents

Chapter 1: The Age Of Intuition

Intuition is the sensation in your stomach whilst you intuitively understand that some element you are doing is accurate or incorrect.

Or it's the instantaneous at the same time as you apprehend compassion, or worry, in every distinctive's face. You don't apprehend why you experience that way; it's simply a hunch.

But what's it? After all, researchers can't see it in the thoughts.

While comprehending intuition gives a terrific problem for technological knowledge, more or less speakme, it includes "determined out reactions that aren't the goods of conscious strategies".

1.1 Moving Into The Era Of Intuition

As the energy of our planet keeps to growth, we're being counseled to awaken our intuitive nature. We are starting to recognise how our thoughts-set itself determines our outer international and our life enjoy.

And as we are going from the age of knowledge to the age of instinct we are outgrowing the antique paradigms of fear, wrath, and alienation. Flipping the script and locating a high-vibrational mind-set that encourages oneness, compassion, love, co-creation, and satisfaction.

Have you ever discovered which you and I are dwelling in a 2nd of transition? The more we learn how to experience our particular vibration and paintings consciously with strength, the extra we are able to improve ourselves and our life. To rent our instinct is to walk into this new second.

Intuition is the capability to advantage records without proper proof, evidence, or conscious reasoning, or with out comprehending how the facts modified into obtained. It means that our attitude is evolving and the manner we enjoy life.

1.2 Intuition development

In the state-of-the-art viewpoint, there may be no beyond, gift, or future. There is definitely one currently. Intuitive recommend will not come through at the same time as you are projecting into the past or the destiny. Intuition arises while you are grounded inside the gift 2nd.

This inner information emerges whilst the mind is plain and now not distracted. With growing/remembering our intuitive nature is to music into the existing second more and more. Our intuition will increase via consciousness, exercising, and non secular improvement.

We are all born intuitive

We all have been born with intuition. It is like a further muscle that we're getting to know a manner to exercise. And isn't always a present. It is innate in us all. All humans are intuitive creatures. Just as we discover ways to adventure a bicycle, we also can discover ways to harness the capacity of our underlying intuitive intuition.

At one time in our lifestyles, we either pork up our intuitive powers or silly our intuitive voice with the useful resource of the usage of focusing at the rational intellect. Making judgments from reasoning in preference to a heart-based totally truely feature.

Listen, take delivery of as true with and look at

Listen to and accept as real with and placed into effect your instinct in your regular existence. As you broaden more huge conscious you switch out to be more capable of tapping into your instinct. You will discover ways to discriminate amongst profound knowledge and your mind babbling. You will have to discover ways to discern the distinction amongst your logical head and your intuitive coronary coronary coronary heart. Your heart is also like a portal for your higher self. Intuition in no manner yells or needs, it arrives effectively and splendor. It in no way causes any damage.

We examine with the resource of experience

Let's perform a amusing exercising. Focus on a question you could need to realize approximately your self or a circumstance. Try to keep it as simple as viable, with a purpose to allow you to collect the clearest response.

Bring yourself into this gift 2nd thru taking a few deep breaths and concentrating to your outside environment. Close your eyes and start asking a question you will want to get help on.

1.3 5 Real-Life Examples

Intuition isn't always logical. It is not the crafted from a sequence of concept strategies that may be shared or defined. Instead, irrespective of the fact that based totally on deep-seated records, the approach seems natural, even intuitive.

And but, despite the fact that instinct is rapid and normally beneficial, it isn't constantly without a doubt correct. The subconscious brain seeks to find out, examine, and hire styles of notion primarily based mostly on experience and the nice estimate.

Paradoxically, intuition appears unknowable. After all, you can't provide an cause behind the cause within the lower back of a spontaneous choice that emerges out of nowhere.

It in fact takes place.

While intuition takes location for your every day life, it's far on occasion maximum obvious inside the judgments of specialists. The expert is based on years of information, stored in subconscious frameworks, to make rapid, outstanding judgments.

1. Dentistry

Healthcare researchers positioned that expert dentists generally rely on instinct to make hard, time-bound judgments. Based on a few years of deeply saved records, picks are made rapid and are usually superior to folks who rely on clean statistics and logical deliberation.

2. Business

Perhaps all at once, some of the international's most prominent entrepreneurs confess to growing judgments based totally on intuition instead of rational, cautious belief.

Out of a sample of 36 CEOs, 80 five% indicated that instinct – within the form of suggestions of thumb (ROTs) – modified into important to their selection-making manner.

The following list comes from the previous president of Lenovo, William Amelio:

Strategic

Focus on a few important picks.

A preference is better than no choice, but don't allow it move too lengthy if it's not functioning.

Trust your instincts.

People

Communicate predominant alternatives automatically and regularly.

Don't tolerate jerks.

Build a group you could consider.

Trust your instincts.

Self

Get comments early and regularly, and act on it.

Earn others' endure in thoughts and self assurance.

Gain credibility thru revealing your flaws.

You have strengths; employ them.

Trust your instincts.

three. The stag hunt sport

Intuition constitutes a important aspect of each paintings and pleasure.

The stag hunt sport consists of technique, recall, and intuition. Players pick out, in thriller, to both collaborate or compete closer to each other.

The use of instinct is related to time constraints, and taught heuristics (each different term for ROTs) play a vital element in winning the game.

4. Stockbrokers

Human intuition is extraordinarily large — a sophisticated capability crucial to our ancestors' survival – yet it could be incorrect.

In an annual match by using The Wall Street Journal, teams competed on how their investments fared. But even as one aspect end up a difficult and speedy of specially in a function expert dealers, the opportunity come to be a tough and fast of reporters selecting their stocks via the toss of a dart.

Intuitively, knowledge must win.

And yet, it appears, that wasn't actual in this example. The contest have emerge as terminated with out rationalization, maximum probably to shop the stockbroker's humiliation.

5. Art

In 1983, Gianfranco Becchina had an wonderful sixth-century sculpture to be had in the marketplace with a startling $10 million price tag. The Getty Museum, having evaluated X-rays, professional proof, and historic information, approved its acquisition amid lots media hoopla.

However, whilst Evelyn Harrison, a recognized professional on Greek sculptures, and Thomas Hoving, former director of the Metropolitan Museum of Art, visited to realize the statue, they found out, instinctively, some aspect modified into amiss.

According to Hoving, it felt "clean," which have become sudden thinking about the 2,000-year-vintage monument had been hauled out of the ground.

And they were correct. While the sculpture became from a studio in Rome, it got here from a forger spherical 1980, instead of a skilled artist from antiquity.

1.Four How Does Intuition Work? Psychology Theories

While we will see human beings's conduct, despite the breakthroughs made in thoughts imaging, we can't – but – see the thinking methods that move on behind the scenes.

What does psychology have to say about instinct, at the same time as most of what takes location in the mind is unseen - like peering on the outside of a black subject?

Many scientists propose a twin-approach speculation – choice-making techniques divided amongst intuitive (experiential or tacit) and analytical (rational or intentional).

In *Blink: The Power of Thinking Without Thinking*, Malcolm Gladwell (2005) depicts the 2 contrasting strategies as blinking, while instinct is hired, and thinking while an assessment is undertaken.

There may be as an awful lot price in the blink of an eye as in months of low priced concept.

Intuition (or blinking) frequently refers to the utility of information that isn't stated and in well-known manner of lifestyles can be characterised as a "hunch" or "ladies's instinct."

When it takes place, it's now not possible to measure or describe, but it's miles there. As with the following idea:

I had a droop there was some factor incorrect; she genuinely didn't appear like herself.

I agree with "the center of intuition or intuitive answers is that they're acquired with little apparent strive, and generally without aware interest. They entail little or no cognitive deliberation."

"Intuition is a sensation of knowing with out understanding how one is privy to" based actually on the subconscious processing of statistics.

Intuitions also will be inclined to be holistic - incorporating mind from severa sources and frequently looking a bounce in questioning based totally on little knowledge.

1.Five Processes concerned in instinct

Herbert Simon's studies inside the Nineteen Fifties on the concept of restrained rationality underlies a good buy of the paintings on intuition. Simon said that human beings generally make judgments – and limit their cognitive burden – based totally on what is appropriate sufficient.

Rather than arriving at complete and first-rate answers, while provided with precise problems, we generally flip to heuristics – or pointers of thumb – that help in generating intuitive judgments.

The use of heuristics is regarded as ubiquitous and the default technique for making judgments.

The method of popularity - a core advanced feature – is also critical to instinct. It seems one in each of a type from distinct areas of the human reminiscence within the mind, capable of lasting in the maximum demanding settings with precision adequate for practical applications.

Intuition appears to depend upon the automation of the selection-making manner.

Newly decided sports activities commonly rely on declarative data; we need to cautiously examine each step or motion. As a quit end result of experience and getting to know, this data becomes computerized or procedural.

Such sports are completed with out conscious interference, maintaining huge processing try to allowing the thoughts to pay interest on extra excessive or freshly found behaviors.

Forward and backward inferences additionally play a vital part in intuition. The records we've got determined out through enjoy lets us forecast, instinctively, in which the ball will fall or why the teenager stumbled and took movement.

Indeed, the big information we increase through the years allows real-global predictions, allowing us to reply rapidly and successfully in situations that maximum human beings have faced often in advance than.

Learning and retrieval are also notably essential to right intuitive techniques.

Having skilled objects and scenes in advance than, we are pretty adept at sample matching to assist our capability to decide and act short and successfully.

For instance, on the equal time as we stroll proper right into a coffee preserve, we recognize a cup as something we have were given visible frequently in advance than. We moreover recognize, intuitively, that it is in all likelihood to be warm and with out problem spilled on an uneven floor.

Intuition appears to originate - like an epiphenomenon – due to the interaction of severa discrete cognitive techniques, in preference to a single one. They collaborate to offer a speedy and green reaction while it is maximum required.

1.6 Is Intuition Important?

In a word, yeah.

Intuition offers a decrease in regular cognitive load and the functionality to react rapidly even as offering self perception in our understanding and preference-making – regardless of the fact that it may defy exam.

Such instinctive questioning may also additionally benefit from, or be restrained by the use of, enjoy.

When we get a take a look at after dinner, we generally have an instinctive experience of its costs, based totally totally on experience. However, this could fail while we're in a overseas country or did not recognize we had inadvertently picked the maximum high-priced wine in the cellar.

Intuition enables us stay to inform the tale with the useful resource of handing over rapid reactions that, generally, deliver a suitable, straight away movement to treatment a condition. Such reactions rely particularly on "cultural capital," mastering great to the milieu wherein we discover ourselves.

While this typically advantages us, it can bring about bias and prejudice in our choice-making – primarily based on religion, cultural, social, ethical, or even political settings – and may need to be resisted with the useful resource of logical questioning.

Indeed, "intuition can be formally knowledgeable". By enhancing the content and environment round our mastering, we may furthermore lean toward more correct and much less biased, intuitive judgments.

1.7 Instinct, Logic, or Intuition?

While intuition is defined as arriving at knowledge with out counting on reason or inference, it differs from intuition.

The latter is hardwired, a far a lot much less flexible, instantaneous reaction to stimuli.

According to Merriam-Webster, intuition is "a specially inheritable and unalterable propensity of an organism to offer a complicated and specialized reaction to outdoor stimuli without the usage of motive."

It is, because of this, in all likelihood to include an lousy lot less tricky or deep processing. Instinct is intrinsic, hereditary, and encoded into our mind's circuitry due to thousands and heaps of years of evolution.

If a lion roars and I am ignorant of it being at the back of me, I leap, flip, and, maximum probably, flee for the hills. This hobby is extra essential than intuitive or highbrow - however maximum likely, there are shades of grey.

Logic is analytical - the reasoned assessment of an hassle. To stop our taxes, we depend on going via each question, filling every subject, and reference spreadsheets, sticky notes, or boxes of receipts. Tax endorse isn't always going to recognise very last touch using an instinctive, gut experience about how a whole lot we owe.

1.Eight Its Role in Decision Making

While we can be in the important oblivious to our every day selection-making, it's miles probably to involve a mixture of intuitive and intentional wondering.

And the significance of intuition seems to be no absolutely one in every of a kind in our each day highbrow strategies than in greater large judgments.

Intuitive choice-making is based on our in advance memories and, as a result, regularly powerful in similar activities, at the same time as preceding consequences and reading had been precious and correct.

Where the winning or future circumstance is significantly wonderful, we want to utilize our intuition with care. Without low priced concept, every movement accompanied is probably unproductive at incredible or unstable at worst.

When it simply works well and time boundaries are stringent, instinct may additionally moreover allow rapid, focused thinking (e.G., the boat is sinking or the bomb is ticking). When there's time to undergo in mind – how are we able to combat worldwide warming or racism? – we want to depend on low priced, evidence-based totally evaluation.

Research on the University of South Wales verified that instinct substantially enhances preference-making at the same time as consisting of that nonconscious know-how might also moreover growth choice correctness, tempo, and self assure.

1.Nine The Link Between Intuition and Creativity

Creativity, like intuition, may be hard to describe.

And yet they each seem to require the interpretation of thoughts into something real, new, and beneficial in expressing thoughts and addressing troubles.

The premise that intuition is perceptual, unconsciously combining unrelated bits of records, additionally implies extremely good interplay with creativity. Both instinct and creativity seem, at some diploma, to synthesize cloth from numerous property into some problem understandable.

A modern-day have a study has discovered out correlations between intuition and the early ranges of the innovative manner, together with idea advent and appraisal tiers.

A Take-Home Message

Intuition is an particularly sturdy tool for selection-making. It ensures we react inside the present, liberating up crucial thoughts belongings to stand glowing events and decorate studying.

While now not infallible, intuition is beneficial.

Intuition gives us a "intestine" reaction - an inner voice –– beyond reasoning or taught answers, displaying both who we are and the information we've got were given have been given received.

If we pay interest, we may additionally make the most of the creativity it gives and the texture of self notion that it gives you. Let intuition assist you increase and make time-crucial judgments based totally on assets that are not usually quite genuinely accessed.

Recognize the situations even as you are at your maximum intuitive. Find opportunities to copy them and hire the functionality for creativity and fast, clever desire-making.

Chapter 2: Optimizing The Subconscious Thoughts

What Is The Subconscious Mind?

Do you bear in mind on the identical time as you tried to journey a bicycle for the primary time?

Can you rely the range of repetitions required to carry out a ideal dance?

Have you ever attempted to understand a modern-day musical tool?

Most possibly, early efforts to synchronize a sparkling set of complex sports activities are typically tough. Once we develop extra adept, these motions start to need an entire lot much less conscious cognizance until the entirety starts offevolved offevolved to drift resultseasily.

All the ones spontaneous actions are pushed via one of the maximum powerful internal forces which govern human behavior - the unconscious thoughts (additionally commonly called the nonconscious thoughts).

2.1 Subconscious Mind: Where Does It Hide?

It's pretty uncommon to listen about conscious and unconscious sorts of sports activities while scientists speak about the mind. As a final results, most people are acquainted with the idea that our behavior is a great deal less low priced than we assume it to be.

Whether we adore it or no longer, our capacity to govern mind, coordinate moves, or feel emotions relies on the volume of information processing.

The belief of higher layers of records processing became created and considerably investigated thru way of famed Austrian psychologist Sigmund Freud (1856 – 1939) who proposed the three-level mind model. According to his concept, the mind might be split into the ones stages:

Three-degree mind version

Conscious - defines all thoughts and behaviors interior our interest. For instance, the beauty and pleasance of the fragrance of a purple tulip

Subconscious - identifies all reflexes and instinctive sports sports we may additionally come to be aware about if we don't forget them. For instance, our capability to pressure a vehicle: as we accumulate revel in we save you thinking about which gears to use, which pedals to push, or which replicate to have a take a look at but can always become aware of what became completed as soon as we reflect onconsideration on it.

Unconscious - characterizes all preceding memories and reminiscences, however at instances unreachable to us irrespective of how tough we strive to hold in thoughts to hold subjects up. For example, the primary phrase we've determined to pronounce, or the way it felt on the way to walk on our very very own.

2.2 SUBCONSCIOUS MIND POWER EXPLAINED

Your unconscious mind is sort of a massive reminiscence keep. It permanently saves everything that ever takes place to you, and its potential is largely endless.

By the time you attain the age of 21, you've already virtually saved multiple hundred times the contents of the whole Encyclopedia Britannica.

Under hypnosis, human beings also can frequently don't forget, with excellent readability, earlier sports activities that transpired a few years earlier.

But why don't we actively bear in thoughts all our unconscious brains?

While your unconscious reminiscence is sort of ideal, it's miles your conscious hold in mind that is dubious.

The first rate data is we are able to employ our conscious brains to reprogram our subconscious minds and harness the energy of great wondering to conquer terrible mind and horrible conduct to carry out all of our existence targets.

Let me show you procedures.

2.Three What Is Your Conscious Mind Vs. Your Subconscious Mind?

The aware mind may be characterized as whatever you're now aware of. What you feel, doing, seeing, touching, experiencing. You are aware about it or aware about it.

Consciousness does not entail stored data. It is what is going on nowadays. It does entail thinking and making judgments. It is easy to manipulate your conscious mind seeing that you could utilize it to create decisions.

In assessment, your unconscious mind is continuously strolling in the historical past, but you are not usually privy to it. Sometimes dubbed the subconscious mind, the subconscious mind consists of all of the recorded facts of the entirety you have got ever encountered.

Because of this, it affects how you react to things, inclusive of why you're shy, lazy, consume too much, or have an addiction. On the remarkable element, your subconscious mind moreover impacts things like why you are pushed, confident, a success, completely satisfied, high quality, and so on.

The trick is the usage of your reputation to constructively have an effect to your unconscious ideas. Learning how to utilize the 2 together is a fantastic tool.

2.Four How Your Subconscious Mind Operates

Every time that you are extensive conscious, your five senses are taking in a regular movement of information. These reviews are stored as memories, as a computer saves statistics. But we do not need to actively remember masses of this understanding. In fact, we probable forget about 90 5-ninety nine% of our ordinary sports activities.

However, we realize those mind and images are however for your thoughts due to the truth hypnosis can deliver again deep memories.

Studies inside the place of psychology on how the brain works show that the testimonies we have an effect on the manner we count on and behave, particularly those in our early infancy. Although you do now not keep in mind maximum of your existence studies, the unconscious records for your mind controls ninety to ninety 5% of your conduct.

Your unconscious mind may be likened to working a jet on autopilot. It is continuously jogging applications to govern how we skip, sit down down, breathe, speak, and so forth. We don't ought to think about those gadgets, they robotically take location for the motive that recognise-a way to perform them is stored to your mind.

Your unconscious thoughts possesses what is termed a homeostatic impulse. It regulates your body temperature at 98.6 degrees Fahrenheit, simply as it keeps you respiratory often and keeps your coronary coronary coronary heart pumping at a specific pace.

Through your autonomic aggravating tool, it maintains a balance some of the masses of chemicals on your billions of cells without a doubt so your entire physical system runs in common concord most of the time.

Your subconscious thoughts additionally practices homeostasis on your highbrow sphere, through retaining you questioning and behaving in a manner consistent with what you have got finished and said inside the past.

Your unconscious mind leads you to experience emotionally and physically uncomfortable whenever you try to do a little thing new or unusual or adjust any of your installed habits of behavior. The sensation of tension and pain are mental indicators that your subconscious has been engaged. But it's been searching for to broaden such behavior patterns in the history prolonged in advance than you'll ever understand such sensations.

The propensity to decide to the ones patterns is one cause why conduct can be so hard to break. However, at the same time as you learn to actively assemble such styles, you may harness the strength of addiction and purposefully set up new comfort zones to which your unconscious will adapt.

You can also moreover feel your mind pushing you lower back closer to your consolation region each time you try a few element new. Even considering doing a little component precise from what you're used to will make you feel annoying and stressful.

This is why developing new behavior to help you acquire your targets, together with following time control pointers, may be difficult to use at the start, however after they become a habit or everyday they may stay to your consolation place. In doing so, you've changed your subconscious to perform on your advantage.

2.Five Changing Habits: Using Your Conscious Mind To Properly Program Your Subconscious Mind

Since your unconscious mind has this form of first-rate diploma of strength over your accurate and horrific movements, the motive is to train your mind to create greater fantastic behaviors.

This is wherein your conscious mind is to be had in. You may moreover employ your recognition to reprogram or retrain your subconscious mind to carry out matters which can be more useful to your planet now and in your destiny.

Do you have got targets you need to gain, behavior that appear hard to interrupt, aspirations for a dream profession so that you can revolutionize your life, or a photo of the future that looks in reality particular from these days?

Using your conscious thoughts to teach your unconscious thoughts also can offer you success in all components of your life which you are striving for.

It starts by way of the usage of following those four steps:

1. Recognize The Roadblock

First, you need to determine what is retaining you decrease again from attaining what you want to do.

What are your limiting thoughts or fears?

For example, in case your ambition is to put in writing a ebook, however you truely can't appear to get commenced or whole it, what's keeping you from sporting out that? Do you worry no one will examine it otherwise you don't have sufficient time otherwise you're no longer a professional creator?

All of these mind are what you be given as authentic with you studied to be actual, but they may be not generally real. Your subconscious thoughts has been taught to act that way, and your aware selections will comply with.

Roadblocks will also be bodily obstructions. Perhaps you need to shed pounds, however you permit your addiction of browsing thru social media for 30 minutes a day occupy the time that is probably spent workout.

Think approximately your desires and aspirations and discover what beliefs, behaviors, principles, or hurdles are blockading you from accomplishing them.

2. Let Go Of Limiting Thoughts

Once you recognize what your limiting mind are, receive them, embody them, and then allow them to move.

Sometimes this desires you to preserve suffering to the surface, into your aware idea, so you may confront it after which release it.

Perhaps you warfare with the potential to increase a trusting courting, for example, however you recognise you in all likelihood did no longer have that modeled that allows you on your teens. When you understand what's the usage of your emotions, you may confront it and find out a higher manner to react.

three. Set Up The Intention With Your Conscious Mind

Now it is time to launch the power of exquisite idea and rewire your subconscious.

Your aware ideas and behaviors may also moreover trade your unconscious thoughts in a heartbeat. A excellent message can also reprogram the manner you experience, heal trauma, and transform styles that make our lives stagnate and bloom into large lives that target the topics that rely maximum.

Use your aware mind to installation anticipation of what will appear in your lifestyles.

For example, on the same time as supplied collectively together with your blockage, say to your self, "Even if I've finished this in the past, I now not do it now."

Your unconscious thoughts will listen, simply because it has listened to all the previous facts it has ever acquired. Over time, your unconscious mind has no choice but to examine. It is no longer interested in preceding conduct as it has determined a modern-day dependancy.

The secret is picturing what you want to stand up, having a method for the way you may reply for your hurdles, the use of your conscious mind to live alert and have a look at what's taking place, and identifying to conform along with your plan in the gift.

4. Let Your Subconscious Mind Take Over

The goal is to in the long run permit your conscious lighten up and allow your subconscious take fee. Once you have got given your unconscious an possibility manner to react, it's going to count on that is the way it want to reply.

With the proper phrase, motion, or concept, you've got got mounted a extremely-present day street on your subconscious thoughts to find out its data banks and find out an outstanding, uplifting, and effective manner to react.

2.6 Positive Tools To Help You Tap Into Your Subconscious Mind

There are numerous matters you may do to reprogram your subconscious thoughts each day. Be proactive thru which encompass them in your ordinary. Here are some of the only strategies to leverage the electricity of your unconscious thoughts together with your conscious efforts.

Positive Affirmations

Your subconscious thoughts makes the entirety you're saying and do in shape a pattern normal with your self-idea, your "grasp software program."

This is why repeating outstanding affirmations are so powerful — you can reprogram your idea styles through slipping in first-class and fulfillment-orientated sound bites.

Start every day with a effective affirmation. Say one every time you're faced with a roadblock or venture. Inspirational Quotes

Reading inspirational expenses is so impactful for human beings dedicated to powerful thinking. By focusing your mind on uplifting terms and ideas, your subconscious will start to implement a powerful sample to your manner of thinking and your outlook on existence.

Apply the equal principle through reading an uplifting article each day, analyzing useful books relevant on your lifestyles goals, listening to instructional or inspirational podcasts, and searching a motivational video or film.

Pareto Principle

In lifestyles, eighty% of the final outcomes of some aspect you do is usually the stop end result of 20% of your common try. This is generally dubbed the Pareto Principle and it's quite sturdy in case you maintain close to it.

Follow this method with the beneficial resource of making sure the devices you accomplish each day are ones with a purpose to have the most important have an impact on on reaching your life dreams. When you make those acts a concern, they not slip thru the gaps, fall sufferer to procrastination, or are swamped thru special sports.

SMART Goals

All your varieties of wondering and doing are stored on your subconscious thoughts. It has remembered all your consolation zones and it strives to keep you in them. This is why it's so critical to make developing SMART goals a normal practice. Over time, preserving busy and centered on all of your goals becomes a part of your consolation quarter.

2.6 Power Of Positive Thinking

Your subconscious mind is subjective. It does now not anticipate or purpose independently; it most effective obeys the guidelines it gets from your conscious thoughts.

Just as your conscious mind can be concept of due to the fact the gardener sowing seeds, your unconscious mind may be checked out due to the truth the garden, or wealthy soil, in which the seeds sprout and thrive.

This is why analyzing the electricity of tremendous questioning is essential to the concept of your whole intellectual device. Your aware mind directs and your unconscious mind obeys.

Consciously select to feed your subconscious with suitable, uplifting ideals.

Habits Of Highly Successful People

For human beings wishing to expand their sphere of comfort zones, I strongly advise exploring the conduct of a success human beings considering the fact that those are the styles usually discovered via the brains of fantastic leaders and thinkers. Unlocking the strength of those conduct will bring you one step inside the route of being able to make the identical matters take place to your life.

These behaviors embody making prepared your day the night time time time before, rating your priority to your to-do list, and finishing your maximum crucial object first.

2.7 Train Your Subconscious Mind To Create Your Best Life

Learning strategies to reprogram your unconscious mind will let you undergo in thoughts in yourself because of the reality that your self warranty will not be threatened via the dread of the unknown. But extra appreciably, doing so will train your mind to be following your real desires, desires, and existence dreams.

The more in touch together with your unconscious you get, the closer you'll be to breaking thru to achievement.

Remember: Taking brief motion for your mind is a crucial detail to fulfillment. Freeing oneself from self-proscribing mind – or doubts – is step one to becoming organized for motion.

2.Eight Scientific Detection of the Subconscious Mind

Up to in the mean time, the capability to give an reason for how the interaction of a couple of tiers of thoughts affects human conduct stays one of the maximum interesting troubles in psychology and neuroscience.

To solve how one degree of thinking influences the other, scientists should emerge as able to understand notable layers of the thoughts.

Quite frequently, the ranges of statistics processing might be recorded using priming paradigms. For example, trendy psychology research discovered how irrelevant signs effect reading and proposed that the impact of conscious, subconscious, and unconscious thoughts can be replicated with the resource of fixing the presentation length of emotive faces.

2.Nine The Subconscious Mind - Study

In this experiment, individuals have been given a series of pictures of human faces and had been requested to assess if the facial features in a previous photograph pondered the identical emotion.

Interestingly, information indicated that individuals had been able to because it have to be determine the difference among facial feelings furnished snap shots were exhibited for at the least zero.047s. Once the time of photos end up shortened to 0.027s - 0.033s, the fee of correct replies plummeted thru approach of virtually half. In assessment, responders have been no longer able to differentiate the facial feelings if the period of the stimulus changed into shortened even similarly - to zero.020s.

In this method, the test established an obvious difference most of the conscious and subconscious consequences of mind: respondents had been first-rate able to post errors-unfastened replies if the photo can also want to reap the extent of conscious attention. More curiously, the length of images, exhibited for so long as zero.027s – 0.033s, couldn't be ok for stimulus verbalization at the extent of aware interest but had

More interestingly, the duration of snap shots, exhibited for so long as zero.027s – 0.033s, couldn't be adequate for stimulus verbalization on the extent of conscious focus but had a detectable impact on behavior.

Specifically, the charge of accurate replies become decreased slightly thru half of, displaying that humans were nevertheless partly capable of deliver the proper responses and suggesting the life of the subconscious mind.

Chapter 3: Unconscious Pressure: A Manner To Detoxify Your Unconscious?

There are some moments in existence that humans find it tough to particular.

This is often the case whether or not or no longer they fall in the area of reputation or the subconscious.

This is the situation of quite a mystery.

If the attention techniques processing with surely one motion at a time, the unconscious will choose to check numerous sports activities concurrently.

Sometimes, and in most situations, this circumstance of things offers rise to strain.

To deal with it, cleaning the unconscious is essential.

While there can be no fantastic technique to have entire manage over this length of your thoughts, you may although act on it thru cleansing.

We display you the manner to carry out it.

three.1 Meditation: the finest way to thoroughly cleanse your unconscious

For efficient purification of the subconscious mind, meditation is a workout that has abundantly set up its usefulness.

It permits to offer you the energy of attention, it truly is critical for conquering your unconscious.

However, to gain success and decrease your pressure stage, it must be deliberate.

To get rid of improvisations, you can begin with the useful resource of specifying a hard and fast time on your intervals.

Usually, five mins is good enough to start an hobby.

And to be more sure, you may use a timer.

Clothing is likewise a essential problem of the effectiveness of your meditation.

The property you placed on must make you revel in comfortable sufficient.

There aren't any greater necessities on this regard except your consolation.

The venue of meditation need to moreover be determined on with consideration.

It must be remoted from any noise to will assist you to higher provide interest in your goals.

People often pick out the terrace in their motel or the parquet.

If you're making all of those settings, then you may be within the occasions vital to meditate correctly.

For higher effect, it is recommended to look at a particular sample.

Begin the hobby with a stretch.

This will will let you lighten up your muscle organizations.

Then lighten up the anxiety during your frame and talk to your ft.

These sports want to put together you for clearing your subconscious.

Subconscious cleaning meditation regimen

The subconscious cleaning meditation is preferably completed while seated.

To gain this, the seat you operate must be sturdy and feature a backrest.

While sitting on it, your feet need to be firmly on the floor.

To enhance this pose, you may also create a bypass together along with your legs.

Your limbs should be placed on a pillow placed on the web site of meditation.

Then elevate your yet again such that your backbone has a completely herbal curve.

Likewise, your forearms need to be positioned parallel to your facets and your elbows, barely bent.

The place of the arms is without a doubt on the knees.

Your chin must be dropped softly to allow your eyes to relaxation on the floor.

This is the pinnacle of the street posture, and also you need to make an effort to preserve it intact at a few degree inside the exercise.

The right exercising begins offevolved with the breath.

Focus on it and do it in fact.

Try to have a have a look at the mind that come into your mind and let them roam at the same time as you relaxation.

As a effect, you'll be capable of get those mind and due to this anxiety, out of your unconscious in your interest.

The preliminary u . S . A . Will therefore be cleared.

What has to be completed next is to take be aware of these thoughts, and get hold of them with out judgment.

Throughout the meditation, your attention should stay focused to your breathing.

Some healthy behaviors to pick out for cleansing the unconscious

If you try to stay useful in your normal life, your unconscious will be swiftly cleared of its anxiety.

Always be first-rate

You need to begin through developing a exercise of being first rate for your speech.

If feasible, update terrible phrases you may say with affirmations.

This irrefutably implies a trade of language which will sooner or later lead you to a alternate of body of mind.

To allow you to achieve this hobby, you could already pick out the topics that drive you to negativity.

Determine your justifications for preserving your incapacity to gain this or that other.

By know-how them, you will be able to better draw close them.

Of direction, exchange will now not come spontaneously, but with attempt and bravery, you can be successful.

Learn to supply a top notch monologue

Still thinking about the behaviors to have, you can, as an instance, assemble an fine incantation personal to you.

It might be a quick announcement or a part of a sentence that might inspire you while anxiety tries to creep in.

You also can moreover then make use of this invocation as a treatment for mind that may demoralize you.

When applied continuously, it frees the subconscious thoughts from its problems and anxiety.

To recite the incantation, preferably, location your hand on a part of your frame that you have chosen.

It can be the stomach or the coronary coronary heart.

It will then be the seat of optimism for your frame.

Concentration and self-self belief are suggested to allow you to simply apprehend the blessings of this interest.

Practice the artwork of visualizing

If you have got troubles with the ones bodily video video games, or inside the event that they have not paid off correctly, you can flip to visualization.

It is a way that pushes you to adopt a intellectual and common workout session of your targets.

This will can help you achieve them quicker, thereby freeing you from dread.

For a start, you can start by using seeing an photo or a familiar item.

To accumulate this, take an interest in each function of the item: colour, texture, posture, and lots of others.

Otherwise, you could additionally bear in mind your recollections or scenes from films.

For this form of illustration, odors and tastes need additionally be considered.

However, you want to set your goals quite actually.

The desires to be reached and all of the elements that go together with them want to steer your vision.

If you've got were given an occasion scheduled, the region, time, and conditions surrounding it want to guide you.

Is it feasible to manipulate to loose your unconscious from subconscious stress?

The answer is unambiguous, yes!

However, you can't accomplish this without placing strain on yourself.

Daily meditation and considering terrific behavior may be of superb beneficial resource to you in obtaining this goal.

Get started out nowadays!

Chapter 4: Unlocking The Third Eye Chakra

The mysteries of third eye activation & the manner it alters your existence

Our 0.33 eye, attention, and popularity all interlinked?

Did you know that there can be an power middle in your body that may boom your hobby, and cognizance, or even deliver up intuitive abilities? You also can have heard many non secular parents talk about waking the 0.33 eye chakra the various 7 chakras within the human frame and their reviews with it.

If a person is targeting their mission, then they could revel in some form of zero.33 eye activation. For instance, at the same time as a cricketer is that specialize of their exercise, whilst they will be constantly considering the game and the way it can be higher, they acquire an intuitive knowledge of in which the subsequent ball goes to attain. A pinnacle cricket participant wouldn't want an analyst to inform them some element, they instinctively understand what's going to appear subsequent.

Even a businessman who is completely focused on their profession, through some manner is aware about how their consumer will reply to a particular proposition or situation. The heightened alpha wave emissions allow people to intuit what also can seem rapidly, linked to the place they will be especially targeted on.

4.1 7 Chakras inside the human frame, Significance & How to balance them

What are the 7 chakras in the human body? How huge are they for us? There are seven chakras or power centers within the human frame through which our essential energy or prana shakti travels. Sometimes, those power pathways are clogged and this results in illness and abnormalities in the body's natural sports activities activities. It is vital to understand what every chakra symbolizes and what we are capable of do to maintain this electricity flowing without troubles. This is feasible at the identical time because the chakras are balanced.

How yoga allows to balance 7 chakras inside the body

When a chakra i.E. Wheel of energy is locked, the motion might also additionally assist the discharge of the prana (power). Yoga postures are a remarkable approach to discharge stale or trapped power from the body due to the fact they welcome new, residing strength again in thru positions and the breath.

The exercise of yoga in the long run leads us to a rustic of concord, it genuinely is viable while we establish a condition in our frame in which strength also can glide freely from the lowest of the spine (the Root Chakra), to and past the top of the top (the Crown Chakra). When power can go along with the float freely through us like manner, we may additionally moreover enjoy a situation of concord with the cosmic power, which runs through all dwelling matters. When every chakra is unblocked, it rotates like a wheel, thus the choice 'chakra' that means 'wheel' in Sanskrit.

Since yoga is each a bodily and non secular issue, yoga postures are not simply exercise sporting activities on your frame but additionally your mind, feelings, and soul, making it the proper exercise for balancing your chakras.

four.2 The 7 chakras within the human body

Let's look at the seven chakras in our body, how they affect the body, what imbalance motives to our persona and organs, and a manner to make it right via the use of balancing the chakras with yoga asanas or postures.

Muladhara Chakra

Swadishthana Chakra

Manipura Chakra

Anahata Chakra

Vishuddhi Chakra

Ajna Chakra

Sahasrara Chakra

1. Muladhara Chakra

Element: Earth

Color: Red

Mantra: LAM

Location: Base of the spine a number of the anus and genitals

How it impacts the frame: The Muladhara Chakra controls the health of the bones, tooth, nails, anus, prostate, adrenals, kidneys, decrease digestive talents, excretory techniques, and sexual hobby.

Imbalance inside the chakra leads to weariness, horrible sleep, lower decrease again ache, sciatica, constipation, depression, immune-related ailments, obesity, and eating issues.

The behavioral impact of the imbalance:

Traits of a balanced chakra:

ungrounded worry

a feeling of being grounded and targeted

anger

experience of dedication and independence

low vanity

electricity and electricity

loss of confidence

power and stillness

obsession with consolation

capability to digest meals well

possessiveness

Poses that balance Muladhara chakra: Grounding-into-toes positions like

Mountain Pose

Side-Angle Pose

Warrior Pose

Standing Forward Bend

Bridge Pose

2. Swadishthana Chakra

Element: Water

Color: Orange

Mantra: VAM

Location: Situated at the lowest of the pubis the numerous genitals and the sacral nerve plexus

How it impacts the body: The Swadishthana Chakra offers with the man or woman's emotional identification, creativity, choice, delight and self-gratification, reproduction, and intimate connections.

It regulates the sexual organs, stomach, pinnacle intestines, liver, gallbladder, kidney, pancreas, adrenal glands, spleen, middle spine, and autoimmune device.

An imbalanced Swadishthana Chakra ends in lower again pain, sciatica, faded libido, pelvic ache, urinary troubles, bad digestion, low resistance to infection and viruses, weariness, hormonal imbalances, and menstruation problems.

The behavioral effect of imbalance:

Traits of a balanced chakra:

irritability

a sense of rate and friendliness

shyness

intuitiveness

guilt

energy

tendency accountable

enjoy of belonging

sexual obsession

specific sense of humor

lack of creativity

Poses that stability Swadhisthana chakra: Hip starting positions like

Standing Wide Forward Bend

Sitting Wide Forward Bend

Bound Angle Pose

3. Manipura Chakra

Element: Fire

Color: Yellow

Mantra: RAM

Location: At the volume of the umbilicus corresponds to the belly or sun plexus

How it influences the frame: Manipura Chakra interacts with a feeling of belonging, and intellectual comprehension of feelings, and determines self-esteem in a person.

It oversees the efficient functioning of the pinnacle belly, gallbladder, liver, middle spine, kidney, adrenals, small intestines, and belly.

An imbalanced Manipura Chakra may additionally moreover furthermore motive diabetes, pancreatitis, adrenal imbalances, arthritis, colon ailments, belly ulcers, intestinal tumors, anorexia/bulimia, or low blood pressure.

The behavioral effect of the imbalance:

Traits of a balanced chakra:

loss of self esteem

lively and assured nature

timidness

intelligence

enjoy of depression

immoderate productivity

worry of rejection

advanced interest

incapacity to make preference

suitable selection

judgemental and irritated nature

hostility

Postures that stability Manipura chakra: Heat-constructing positions like

Sun Salutation Pose

Warrior Pose

Backbends like Bow Pose

Twists like Sitting Half-spinal Twist

Abdominal-strengthening postures encompass Boat Pose

4. Anahata Chakra

Element: Air

Colors: Green or pink

Mantra: YAM

Location: On the cardiac plexus in the location of the coronary heart

How it affects the frame: Anahata Chakra impacts a person's social identity and affects attributes like keep in mind, forgiveness, unconditional love, data, compassion, and worries of the soul.

It relates to the functioning of the coronary heart, rib cage, blood, circulatory gadget, lungs and diaphragm, thymus gland, breasts, esophagus, shoulders, hands, and hands.

An imbalance also can moreover create troubles related to the thoracic spine, pinnacle decrease again and shoulder problems, bronchial allergies, coronary heart abnormalities, shallow breathing, and lung ailments.

The behavioral impact of the imbalance:

Traits of a balanced chakra:

hassle with love

the sensation of completeness and wholeness

loss of want, rate and self notion

compassion

feeling of despair

empathy

temper variations

friendliness

optimism

extended motivation

outgoing nature

Postures that stability Anahata chakra: Chest-openers like

Camel Pose

Cobra Pose

Fish Pose

Pranayamas like Alternate Nostril Breathing or Bellow breath

5. Vishuddhi Chakra

Element: Sound or Ether

Color: Blue

Mantra: HAM

Location: On the quantity of the neck, the nerve plexus of the pharynx vicinity

How it affects the body: Vishuddhi Chakra interacts with man or woman attributes which encompass conversation, creativity, religion, honesty, self-popularity, and expression.

It regulates the throat, the thyroid, and parathyroid gland, the trachea, cervical vertebrae, vocal cords, the neck and shoulders, hands, fingers, esophagus, mouth, teeth, and gums.

An imbalanced Vishuddhi Chakra produces thyroid dysfunctions, sore throat, stiff neck, mouth ulcers, gum or teeth problems, laryngitis, and listening to impairments.

The behavioral effect of the imbalance:

Traits of a balanced chakra:

shaken religion

improved creativity and expressiveness

indecisiveness

powerful communication abilities

susceptible will electricity

contentedness

loss of expressiveness

particular listening competencies

lack of creativity

proneness to dependancy

Postures that stability Vishuddhi chakra:

Fish Pose

Cat Stretch

Neck stretches like Balasana and Supported Shoulder Stand

Bridge Pose

Plow Pose

6. Ajna Chakra

Element: Light

Colors: Indigo

Mantra: AUM or OM

Location: Between the eyebrows (1/three eye)

How it affects the body: Ajna Chakra offers with self-reputation, know-how, intelligence, clairvoyance, execution of mind, detachment, insight, comprehension, and intuitive reasoning.

It regulates the sports activities of the mind, eyes, listening to, nostril, pituitary gland, pineal glands, and the neurological device. Any imbalance could possibly lead to migraines, nightmares, eyestrain, reading impairments, panic, unhappiness, blindness, deafness, seizures, or spinal dysfunctions.

The behavioral effect of the imbalance:

Traits of a balanced chakra:

lousy judgment

smooth thinking

confusion

wholesome imagination

worry of reality

robust intuition energy

indiscipline

specific recognition

attention problems

improved interest

proneness to dependancy

Postures that stability Ajna chakra:

Child Pose

Meditation

Seated Yoga Mudra

Eye physical video video games embody palming the eyes and rotational grazing

7. Sahasrara Chakra

Element: Conscience

Colors: Violet or White

Mantra: Silence

Location: Crown of the pinnacle

How it influences the frame: Sahasrara Chakra promotes intuitive knowledge, connection to spirituality, integration of thoughts-body-spirit, and conscious recognition.

It oversees the middle of the pinnacle and midline above the ears, brain, neurological system, and pineal gland.

An imbalance within the Sahasrara Chakra produces continual tiredness and sensitivity to light and sound.

The behavioral effect of the imbalance:

Traits of a balanced chakra:

lack of motive

a experience of oneness with the universe

identity catastrophe

open mindedness

disbelief in any spiritual practices or devotion

intelligence

lack of concept

thoughtfulness

revel in of fear

receptivity to thoughts and mind

materialistic nature

an everyday harmonious individual

Postures that balance Sahasrara chakra:

Balancing postures like Tree Pose that increase hobby of the body

Yoga Mudra

Imbalance is a part of existence, but, the commonplace exercise of yoga asanas allow you to stability your chakras, allowing you to live a glad, pleased, and satisfied lifestyles in the red of fitness!

four.Three How mind waves are associated with our 1/3 eye

The zero.33 eye, to understand from a non secular attitude, is the agya chakra or 1/3 eye chakra. There are seven energy facilities in our body in which nerve elements intersect. The agya chakra is the energy aspect discovered in the center of our eyebrows (pineal gland). This element is related to the capability to hit upon things past the five senses, frequently referred to as intuition.

The agya chakra is related to the frame's pituitary and hypothalamus glands. Our mind generates splendid waves while it is experiencing various things:

1. Beta waves are launched even as you go through grief, loss, anxiety, or ache.

2. Alpha waves are released whilst we revel in peace, relaxation, and immoderate satisfaction. Alpha waves have quieter vibrations and perform as sonar.

Dolphins are recognised to comprise a excessive quantity of alpha wave function in their brains and this lets in them to navigate within the water. Their sonar capabilities similarly to a submarine. Physically, the softness of the pituitary and thoughts glands permits the alpha waves to unfold.

Did you understand?

In youngsters, the pituitary and hypothalamus glands are exceedingly touchy which makes it viable for them to be more observant and intuitive. As we come to be older, the glands get rigid and a few calculus is fashioned spherical them, the power and frequency of the alpha wave manufacturing lessen.

3. Gamma waves are the maximum powerful and can great be professional in a profound meditation country, furthermore known as samadhi.

Our mind emits alpha waves while the frame is aligned with nature. When one is in concord with nature thru their acts and thoughts, their whole lifestyles seems like it is part of the universe. Because of this, nature communicates nice subjects to a person who is experiencing strong alpha wave hobby. Commonly, that is termed instinct.

"Third eye is same to intuition. It grows even as you're extra grounded and content cloth."

- Gurudev Sri Sri Ravi Shankar

The feeling of gamma wave emission takes place in our subtle body and best even as we enjoy commonplace alpha wave emissions. Gamma-ray emissions cause the agya chakra. When the zero.33 eye engages, we feel a sensation of lightness in our questioning.

4.Four How might also we experience 1/three eye activation?

Meditation is one of the techniques. Do we revel in 1/three eye activation out of doors of meditation? Yes!

Whenever a person is very centered, and if they may be completing their paintings with maximum willpower and attention, then their 0.33 eye turns on, particularly for that element of their lifestyles.

It additionally works in opposite. If a person is meditating or appearing special strategies to activate their 0.33 eye (pineal gland 0.33 eye), they'll be located to experience superior attention and consciousness inside the artwork that they're engaged in.

How to open your zero.33 eye?

The spiritual sports that assist wake up the 1/three eye are:

Meditation

Nadi Shodhan Pranayama

Padma sadhana

These workout routines ease our minds and assist us emerge as tuned with nature. As the mind settles down, the mind function improves and the alpha waves start emitting. Due to this, we experience extended interest and attention of the subjects we are appearing. This chronic focus turns on the zero.33 eye.

According to Gurudev, "Too masses food, an excessive amount of sleep, and too much workout are unfavourable to development in our intuitive potential."

People who automatically experience zero.33 eye activation understand a distinction inside the way their breath moves. Usually, it's miles said that the charge of our respiration is haphazard and it each flows from the left or proper nostril. People who revel in third eye activation take delivery of as real with that their breath is in particular deep and centered.

This happens quite grade by grade and if you experience 1/three eye activation then you may revel in that your breath is flowing quite centrally.

four.Five Experiences of one/3 eye chakra activation

Alpha wave emissions bring about the mind being calmer and more focused. Whether one is a scholar, businessman, artist, or a non secular seeker, one may experience an splendid shift of their existence with sports that cause 1/three eye activation and on the identical time as it activates. Some of the encounters consist of:

Better interest span, which has substantially advanced from in advance than. Their hobby to detail and interest additionally upward thrust dramatically.

They moreover be given as right with that their senses end up mainly eager, giving them a heightened reputation of what takes location in their environment. The revel in of sight, being attentive to, and taste are idea to get sharper.

Initially, agya chakra activation may result in inflammation and temper troubles. But this sense is similar to washing the carpet while the accrued dust comes out . Once they reduce, you will phrase that you are feeling at peace and anger doesn't have an effect on you as it did previously. Continuous reviews of 0.33 eye activation cause a sensation of profound peace in the thoughts.

One of the maximum enjoyable markers of 0.33 eye activation is the sensation of willpower. Usually, people claim that willpower is an enjoy of the coronary heart and focus is the potential of the thoughts. However, zero.33 eye activation effects in the feeling of actual willpower. It is probably aimed inside the course of an art form, a topic, or a workout however regularly, it is towards divinity.

four.6 What is the call of the sport of the 0.33 eye?

The secret of zero.33 eye activation: The 1/three eye from a spiritual perspective is the agya chakra or third eye chakra. There are seven power centers in our frame wherein nerve elements intersect.

The agya chakra is the energy trouble positioned in the center of our eyebrows (pineal gland) (pineal gland). It is associated with the notion past the 5 senses, additionally termed intuition. The 1/3 eye is related to the body's pituitary and hypothalamus glands.

4.7 What occurs whilst your third eye chakra opens?

When your 1/3 eye chakra opens, it boosts your interest, and attention and additionally brings up intuitive abilities. It brings a sensation of lightness to our brains.

How can making a decision whether or not your third eye is open?

If you are finishing your paintings with utmost hobby and awareness, then you could be assured that your zero.33 eye is engaged or open, specially for one element of your existence.

four.Eight Can you revel in your chakras open?

Yes, we're able to feel our chakras open. The tingling sensation, extra interest span, acute perceptions, and feeling of dedication suggests the hole of a chakra.

Chapter 5: Building Your Intuition Inventory

18 Ways To Develop & Strengthen Your Intuition

We stay in a worry-based totally society that obsesses on trying to manipulate existence. We're afraid of uncertainty, so we are continuously predicting the whole thing that may work incorrect and doing all internal our power to defend in competition to eventual tragedy.

It's an arduous way to stay, and it is able to result in a persistent circumstance of anxiety, fear, and tiredness. Luckily, you do now not want fear to defend yourself due to the reality you have got were given instinct—a sturdy internal know-how.

We are all gifted with an intuition that is powerful, honest, and perfectly attuned to our actual route. Whether you placed it to apply or no longer is as a top notch deal as you. Here are some techniques to dial up the extent on that sincere inner voice:

1. Meditate.

Messages out of your intuition have a propensity to be quiet, so spending time in solitude will assist you listen and examine those messages.

2. Start looking at the entirety that you could along with your 5 conventional senses.

Doing so may additionally additionally enhance your sensitivity on your sixth revel in.

3. Pay interest for your desires.

When the cognitive thoughts is preoccupied, it can overwhelm the intuitive proper mind and the unconscious mind, the supply of intuition. But at the identical time as you're sleeping, your cognitive mind relaxes and opens room for the unconscious thoughts to signal you through dreams.

4. Get inventive.

Engaging in modern pastimes, which include sketching, scrapbooking, or loose-flow writing quiets the cognitive mind and lets in your intuition to talk out.

5. Consult oracle gambling cards.

Learn to make use of a tarot deck, or attempt a deck of oracle playing cards, and interpret the cardboard's meanings for yourself earlier than you're trying to find advice from a manual.

6. Test your hunches.

Got a sense of which horse will win at the track? Getting a slump that it will rain the next day even supposing the climate prediction says it is able to not? Do you honestly recognize your extremely good pal's new man is horrible records? If you've got were given had been given thoughts about what may additionally need to manifest in the destiny, jot down your hunches, then confirm them in some time. See how frequently you've got been correct.

7. Consult your bodily compass.

Your intuition talks to you through your body, and the more you boom somatic hobby, the greater receptive you grow to be. If you enjoy an ugly bodily sensation at the equal time as you are seeking to make a preference, pay interest.

Do you experience slight or heavy? Got a terrible sensation to your gut? Saddled with a headache or diarrhea? It may honestly be the made from pressure reactions because of wrong anxiety, however it may moreover be your intuition ringing loud and easy.

8. Escape out of your regular normal.

Get away. Slow down. Go on a retreat, take a sabbatical, or really spend an afternoon in unexpected surroundings with now not some thing scheduled. When you are especially busy, it's miles difficult to be alert to the slight phrases of instinct. Try emptying it gradual table and notice in case your intuition pipes up.

9. Spend time in nature.

Being within the herbal surroundings, faraway from era and the cognitive thoughts's special temptations, can also moreover open up the sort of intuition we required whilst we as a species lived exterior and depended upon it to maintain us secure from the weather, predators, and other real frightening risks.

10. Learn from the beyond.

Recall a horrible stumble upon out of your statistics, especially a few problem pretty present day. Before this incidence passed off, reflect on if you obtained any feelings that informed you to maintain away. Maybe you obtained a gut sensation that some element wasn't right.

Maybe you expert a foreshadowing dream or a imaginative and prescient. If so, did you pay heed to that sensation, dream, or imaginative and prescient, or did you argue yourself out of it? Try to hold in mind exactly how you felt. Recall as many facts as possible. The more you may are available contact with the part of you that tried to provide you with a warning, the greater you will be given as actual with it next time.

eleven. Feel more, assume a good deal less.

The mind thinks, constantly talking away, disputing with itself like a loopy person. Intuition, however, feels. If you're now not high excellent whether or not you are listening to your scared thoughts or your sincere instinct, test if you can separate whether or not you're thinking or feeling.

12. Engage in repeated motion.

Run. Dance. Chop carrots. Play the piano. Paint. These physical sports may additionally lighten up the cognitive mind and open up your instinct.

13. Align together collectively along with your beliefs.

Your thoughts may additionally take you away from your integrity, but your intuition never will. Become acquainted with the way you revel in even as you're compromising your beliefs, and you will discover what intuition does now not revel in like. Learn what it looks as if to behave in concord at the side of your values, and you could begin to apprehend your intuition more actually.

14. Practice feeling into human beings in advance than you recognize them.

See what shape of expertise you could gain with the aid of manner of manner of seeing people and experiencing their power signature in advance than you talk to them or studies some thing about them from precise humans. The extra you pay hobby, the extra you will discover you know things you could not probable understand with the cognitive mind.

15. Read books on a way to boost your instinct.

sixteen. Train your instincts.

You may additionally additionally moreover look at instinct in traditional school room environments, in addition to online programs.

17. Release your resistance.

Don't label yourself insane whilst you get maintain of an intuitive instinct. Often, the conscious mind disputes with instinct in vicinity of accepting it. By doing this, you could provide an cause of your self out of an intuitive knowledge that could remodel your existence for the higher.

18. Start a current breathwork exercising.

Breathwork, the practical manipulation of the breath, may additionally additionally moreover provide crucial insights very speedy.

Chapter 6: Teaching Your Thoughts To Believe Your Intestine

Gut Feelings Are Real, but Should You Really 'Trust Your Gut'?

A sixth experience, slump, or gut feeling: Whatever you want to name it, the unexpected flash of expertise from deep internal might also encourage masses of consider.

The conventional expression "consider your gut" refers to following the ones sensations of instinct, frequently as a method to live dependable to oneself.

Following your instinct also can sincerely take you towards the brilliant route for you. And but, you can fear if you ought to place a lot reliance on a sensation, an instinct you could't describe.

Wouldn't clinging to common feel and motive help you are making better choices?

Not continually. Science says instinct may be a beneficial device in positive instances.

It appears that gut sensations advise something, and they may frequently assist you are making extremely good alternatives.

What do 'gut feelings' sincerely sense like?

Ever had a persistent sensation of discomfort approximately a situation? Suddenly enjoy suspicious about a person you in reality met? You can't provide an reason behind your sensations intellectually, but you apprehend some aspect isn't pretty right.

Or possibly a surge of confirmation or calm washes you after a traumatic desire, telling you that you're doing the right problem.

Gut sentiments may furthermore produce some of reviews, a few alternatively similar to the physical signs and signs and symptoms and symptoms associated with worry. Other, greater favorable research can appear to validate your preference.

Some human beings describe gut sensations as a chunk internal voice, however you'll frequently "pay attention" your gut communicate to you in particular methods.

6.1 Signs of a gut sensation

a flash of readability

tension or stiffness for your frame

goosebumps or prickling

belly "butterflies" or nausea

a sinking feeling in the pit of your stomach

sweaty hands or ft

thoughts that keep returning to a certain man or woman or scenario

emotions of serenity, protection, or satisfaction (after you make a decision)

These sentiments usually have a tendency to go lower back on abruptly, however they aren't necessarily immoderate or overpowering.

You might also need to recognize them as a faint whisper or the barest sensation of tension, but they will moreover appear so overwhelming, you could't fathom ignoring them.

If it looks as if your mind is pushing you to be aware of those sensations, well, you're not a ways off the mark.

6.2 Where do they originate from?

Though intestine sensations frequently appear to come out of nowhere, they aren't random. They don't genuinely begin for your belly, each.

The intestine-thoughts link makes it viable for emotional sports to take area as gastrointestinal soreness. When you feel anxious, afraid, or happy that some thing's amiss, you may suffer belly twinges, soreness, or nausea. That's wherein the phrase "gut feeling" originates from.

Experts have provide you with a few doable motives for those sentiments.

Normal mind strategies

Research ties these flashes of instinct to precise mind functions, which incorporates studying and decoding emotional and other nonverbal records.

As you skip approximately your day, your thoughts absorbs and analyses sensory enter out of your environment. You're nicely privy to a number of this statistics.

For example, in case you spot people yelling and shoving every distinctive outside a enterprise agency definitely earlier, you'll probable bypass the road. But you wouldn't claim your gut delivered about you to relocate, because of the fact you made a reasoned preference based on to be had data.

Your thoughts includes out those strategies robotically to help prepare you for any event that would stand up.

Since the ones processes display up inside the "historical beyond," you can no longer generally understand what you're searching or what it signifies.

What if you all at once have a strong impulse to move the road? There's no obvious cause for your inclination, but you could't forget about about it, or the tingle inside the lower again of your neck.

A few seconds even as you move, the be a part of up the constructing ahead comes tumbling down, genuinely wherein you may have been on foot. You appearance in astonishment, heart pumping. How did you understand that might seem?

This burst of notion probable doesn't correspond to 3 supernatural 6th feel. It's extra probably that whilst you went, you made a few unconscious observations.

Maybe one corner of the sign hung unfastened, wobbling in the wind and smacking in competition to the shape. Perhaps exclusive pedestrians determined and walked out of the course, and you located with out figuring out it.

6.Three Predictions based mostly on experience

You can also think about gut sensations as a form of prediction based totally on reports. Even stories you don't in fact don't forget, or understanding you aren't consciously aware about, may also additionally have an impact on you.

A 2016 study that tried to diploma instinct tested this concept:

Researchers requested pupil individuals to stare at a display of small transferring dots and pick whether or not or not the dots traveled inside the path of the right or left facet of the display.

At the equal time, the researchers moreover showed individuals snap shots supposed to generate happy or terrible emotions: a canine, a little one, a rifle, and a snake. These snap shots indicated which direction the dots had been travelling on the show.

Participants best appeared these pictures with one eye, however they weren't conscious they have been viewing them. They decided the dots via a replicate stereoscope, a tool that enabled researchers to exclude such photographs from their conscious notion.

When individuals "determined" those visuals, their picks were faster and further accurate. Skin conductance responses, which measure physiological arousal, imply the people furthermore replied to the visuals physical — in spite of the truth that they in no way identified what they were searching at.

Consider those times of methods modern information — even if you aren't aware about it — could probably provoke intestine responses.

A bunch of buddies invite you to supper at a exquisite eating place. Something tells you no longer to wait, and also you skip on the invite.

A few days later, you concentrate that nearly all people who went fell unwell with food infection. That's even as you don't forget reading a grievance of the eating place that pointed out numerous unclean meals education tactics.

Or you connect to a person on a web dating app and meet in character after a few weeks of messaging. Things begin excellent, however suddenly you sense uneasy, however you can't inform why.

Eventually, you give an explanation for you're no longer feeling properly and depart. Back home, seeking to piece out what took place, you have a observe lower back via their profile and early messages.

Some of the statistics — their preceding employment, in which they went to school, how their last relationship ended — truely contrasts with what they said at the date. You didn't phrase the falsehoods inside the suggest time, but they although functioned as crimson flags to wave you off.

6.Four Gut sensations vs. Tension and paranoia

Gut sentiments deliver up a number of the same physical sensations as fear, so it could be complex to tell the 2 apart. You can also worry your mistrust of a person shows paranoia.

Let's believe you tell a buddy about what transpired on your date in desire to going into those texts. "Your anxieties have been given the excellent of you," they spoke back knowingly. "It's without a doubt herbal to be frightened at the same time as you ultimately meet a person exquisite."

You had been glad a few trouble wasn't right approximately them, but you finish your troubles have to have originated from anxiousness in any case.

Here are some guidelines for differentiating amongst gut sensations, worry, and paranoia.

Gut instincts manual you on a easy course

That sensation of knowledge you discover as a intestine feeling has an inclination to show up in remarkable times or at the equal time as thinking about a positive individual. This intuition typically guides you inside the direction of a clean desire or movement.

Anxiety, rather, has a bent to pay attention on the destiny and usually has much less specificity.

With anxiety, you may find out yourself demanding approximately all types of troubles, specifically ones you can't modify or manipulate. You must give you various mind to address capability unpleasant activities but no longer enjoy assured about any of them.

Paranoia isn't based totally on fact

Paranoia is an unreasonable distrust of human beings and their behavior. You may additionally need to revel in persuaded a person dreams you damage, however you haven't any motive to distrust them and no evidence to back your fears.

These sentiments generally display themselves in numerous settings at some point of your life. In exceptional phrases, you possibly acquired't suspect really one individual.

You might not recognize right away what inspired a gut sensation, however time and hobby may additionally moreover result in greater knowledge, even proof — surely as the evidence, you positioned to your date's communications.

To study the sensation, undergo in thoughts asking your self questions like, "What mainly upsets me about this person or scenario?" or "Has something like this took place before?"

Anxiety stays

Gut sentiments will be predisposed to disappear even as you make a choice. You should even recognise a enjoy of treatment or serenity has changed them.

Anxiety is extra than a transitory temper, however. It frequently places you on continual alert for viable risks. When you cope with one problem, you may start considering a few issue else or start to question your choice.

No rely what you do or wherein you bypass, that non-stop facts rumbling of fear and ache follows.

6.Five When want to you trust your intestine?

Gut sensations may be quite actual topics, anchored in statement and enjoy. Still, you may now not need to make use of them to make every desire.

Here's a have a have a look at some conditions even as following your instinct is commonly a secure bet.

When you may distinguish them from wishful questioning

Wishful questioning is while you want some component to show up so desperately, you begin to recall it's going to show up.

Say you've usually favored to post a ebook, however you only have a few chapters completed. But you sincerely recognize — on your gut — your work is robust sufficient to seize the attention of an editor.

They'll reply speedy, prepared for extra, you guarantee your self. When you deliver an cause of you're looking to squeeze writing in amid the pressures of ordinary lifestyles, they'll provide an enhance that allows you to take time without work and art work to your e-book. In the end, you mail the chapters out and start composing a letter of resignation for the method.

It's hard to rely on intuition even as you lack the recognize-how to all over again it up. Your ambition to be posted clashes with the fact that only some first-time writers get compensated to complete writing a book.

When you want to make a short choice

Research indicates the richness of enjoy formerly cataloged on your thoughts might also moreover assist you well even as you need to decide some trouble suddenly.

Sometimes you'll need to evaluate opportunities, have a look at opinions, or collect as many info as feasible. In distinctive instances, however, you can not have an entire lot time to contemplate.

Say you're seeking out an rental. The location appears awesome, the constructing quiet, and the flat itself is cute. You like it, however you'd want to spend extra time analyzing any defects or negatives in advance than making up your mind.

As you finish your excursion, the proprietor adds, "It's yours if you need it, but I actually have 4 one-of-a-kind humans geared up, so I can simplest provide you with approximately 10 mins to determine."

If your intestine says "Yes! Rent it. This is the location!" you're likely steady to listen. But if this is your first time choosing a domestic for your very very own, it can be most beneficial to have a piece extra enjoy below your belt first.

When you're searching out to get in touch along with your necessities

Logic and reason can't generally take a look at collectively along with your instinctive focus of what you need. After all, you recognize your self best.

Tonight is your pal's birthday party, but you don't want to attend. You enjoy exhausted and spent, and a loud, packed collecting looks like the worst viable region to spend your night time.

Even while you can experience a chunk better when you're there, an internal voice argues, "No way."

Go in advance and bypass it (really). Listening on your body will can help you make selections that help your needs inside the imply time.

When you lack facts

Gut feelings can't update cold, tough proof, however you may now not commonly have statistics to undergo in mind. Or you could have some records, but not sufficient to direct you to an answer.

Perhaps you're looking to pick out amongst manner gives that appear quite identical on paper, or locating out whether or not or now not or not to move on a 2nd date with someone you sense much less than captivated with.

Your emotions can play an important feature in alternatives, so be given as actual with them. The desire you are making could probably resonate greater soundly together with your feel of self.

The bottom line

Time and exercising can hone your instinct, so deliver your gut emotions the eye they deserve. Tuning in to your emotions and body clues also can assist you exercise listening to your gut and studying even as to believe it.

When you war to apprehend gut emotions or have a difficult time distinguishing them from demanding mind, a therapist will let you gather the functionality to tell them aside.

Crystal Raypole has formerly labored as a author and editor for GoodTherapy. Her topics of hobby embody Asian languages and literature, Japanese translation, cookery, natural sciences, intercourse positivity, and mental health. In specific, she's dedicated to helping lessen the stigma surrounding highbrow fitness issues.

Chapter 7: Tips For Building Trust In Yourself

Trust also can help convey us in the direction of different humans. Trusting others, at the aspect of family human beings and buddies, may additionally reassure us that we'll be supported whilst we want it. It's the middle of every proper connection – along with the relationship you have got had been given with your self.

Trusting your self may additionally additionally furthermore growth yourself guarantee, make it an awful lot much less tough a remarkable way to make choices, and reduce your stress stages. And the exceptional records is that even if you don't preserve in thoughts yourself in recent times, with little paintings you can growth that self perception through the years.

7.1 Tips for gaining be given as authentic with in oneself

There's no person greater important to simply accept as proper with than yourself. Sometimes we lose notion in ourselves once we make a mistake or on the identical time as someone criticizes us seriously or continually. It is probably greater tough to make choices while you could't take delivery of as proper with yourself due to the truth you fear you'll make the incorrect opportunity. Or you will be more vulnerable to criticize your personal picks whilst you purpose them to.

Building faith in oneself also can help growth your decision-making skills and self-self assurance. This also can make existence appear a bit plenty less difficult and masses more amusing. Here are a few techniques to help you learn how to accept as true with your self:

1. Be yourself

If you worry about how others will have a look at you or determine you, you may discover it difficult to be yourself with terrific human beings. Acting like a wonderful person than who you're is a symptom that you're lacking self-self notion and notion in your self. Other humans might be capable of understand that.

So how will you constructing up your believe enough to be yourself amongst others? When you begin to experience involved round others, inform yourself that it's OK to be you. Start by manner of the use of working in the course of in the course of the human beings you experience maximum comfortable with, along with your friends and near loved ones. Take be aware in case you experience inclined or uncomfortable and maintain spending time with these folks till your uneasy feelings begin to use up.

Once you may be your self with special human beings, they'll address you with more recall. This might also moreover help you boom your faith in yourself.

2. Set suitable goals

Often, we purpose excessive with our objectives. Instead of seeking to earn $50,000 a one year from our employment, we aspire to make $one hundred,000. Instead of striving to complete a undertaking in weeks, we attempt to accomplish it in a unmarried week. And setting our desires excessive is probably an super trouble because it stimulates us to paintings hard for what we desire.

Unfortunately, growing excessively bold targets has a massive drawback. When we don't obtain our maximum crucial objectives, we go through failure. Failing regularly may weaken your self-self guarantee and capability to don't forget yourself.

Instead of having one primary purpose, keep in mind making numerous tiny goals that lead you in the course of your most important purpose. Doing so will make your huge reason greater possible. You'll additionally accumulate self perception and faith in your self whilst satisfying the little obligations alongside the road.

three. Be mild to yourself

You've actually heard the expression "unconditional love." Maybe it's been addressed regarding the relationship a discern has with their child or the affection that exists among siblings, buddies, or maybe romantic partners. But did you understand that it's moreover incredibly vital to like oneself unconditionally?

Loving oneself unconditionally implies disposing of terrible thoughts about your self and any self-complaint whilst you're making a mistake. Start thru keeping a cautious test in your inner voice, and how it responds for your sports.

Is it top notch or recommend? Is it accepting or critical? When you can love your self unconditionally, you could bear in mind yourself unreservedly. And that develops self belief.

4. Build to your strengths

Everyone is better at positive subjects and poorer at others. You likely have a first rate revel in of what stuff you excel in and which ones you don't carry out as properly with. Trusting oneself implies being capable of try to perform all kinds of subjects with out condemning your self too drastically.

However, if you're seeking to set up religion in your self, it is probably great to do extra of the topics which you're first-rate at and plenty less of the matters that you aren't brilliant at.

If you're no longer first rate what you're exceptional at, ask those human beings closest to you. Spend more time doing the ones activities and developing your take delivery of as proper with understanding you'll reap fulfillment at the ones topics. Be accepting of your strengths, further in your flaws.

five. Spend time with oneself

When you don't receive as true with yourself, you can sense uncomfortable spending time looking inner. You can try to stay occupied all day through commonly becoming immersed in sports or considering tiny things outside of oneself. Break the tendency of looking at a protracted manner from yourself with the useful resource of way of frivolously looking into it.

Chapter 8: What Is The Third Eye?

What is the Third Eye?

Across one among a type religions and practices in the global, the 1/3 eye has many meanings. In present day, it's miles considered a idea that has a wonderful mystical tremendous to it. It is used to provide an cause of a belief that exists beyond seeing with certainly your eyes. Some people take a look at with the zero.33 eye as a form of 'meta' organ. It uses the thoughts, as well as the facts collected from all the senses, to are searching for out styles and new perceptions of the sector. In this manner, you gain perception that you didn't have before and a deeper knowledge of the subsequent steps which you want to take in your existence.

The 1/three eye has been a paranormal concept for hundreds of years. Very few human beings have stated this power and that they kept it a mystery for extremely lengthy. It has widely been a misrepresented and misinterpreted idea.

The third eye is the most eloquent deliver of intuitive focus. A power simplest possessed via manner of the yogis, psychics and fortune tellers in the past. If you meditate and open your zero.33 eye then you can get insights, in advance warnings of danger and excessive diploma of intelligence on the time. The key-word to obtain this purpose is meditation.

For centuries, the occultists and the religious masters have referred to as it the 'seat of the soul'. Once you are capable of open your 1/3 eye, the difference many of the fact and truth becomes crystal clean. You are capable of join your self with the better power place and experience what's impossible to experience in every one-of-a-kind manner. Getting very immoderate intuitive energy is every distinct detail of it. You end up quite aware and set up a connection with your environment. Your intestine feeling gets more potent. Your 6th enjoy starts offevolved operating predominantly.

Your perception of suitable and horrible will change. You can see matters deeply and not from the superficial diploma. You react in a different way and in a far-matured way. This is a totally new feeling. It is like an highbrow looking at the immature quarrels of the youngsters.

Seeing the Third Eye

To apprehend the eye features, allow us to check the way that it's far probably to make use of the Third Eye and translate power. It is expected to view Motion (as an example, a vehicle transferring), Action (you using the automobile), and Exchange of Energy (burning off the fuel). Insert in our capability of projecting & sensing potential (being able to forecast in which the car goes relying on the streets and records the motorist), Quite only concerning wherein electricity, motion, and actions will circulate time past regulation. Add all this together into an inner seen map, and then you definately absolutely've absolutely enlarged the wonderful manner to view Energy gambling (the outcomes of walking with the auto/fuel/goal to push you up the mountain). By viewing strength, it becomes a assets of manner of existence, which we also can furthermore discover the way to interact and experience internal a way.

The Powers of an Open Third Eye

Freedom from Anxiety, Stress, and Worries

With every meditation consultation, your recognition degree increases. You will begin reaching higher states of reputation. The light internal you illuminates you. It takes away your insecurities and fears. Our issues are a crafted from our worldly burdens. With every step we absorb our lives, the Karma has its impact. It keeps on piling up. We fail to understand the effect of Karma and preserve fretting over the results. Meditation offers us the strength to ponder upon our moves and the following Karma. Clear thoughts supply starting to reasoning. We furthermore begin giving weight to purpose and now not without a doubt the effects. This permits in balancing the effect of Karma.

The illumination additionally makes you understand the significance of diverse matters in existence. You can prioritize things higher.

We do many stuff without putting in easy priorities. This creates masses of backlash in shape of pending loan, scholar loan, or unpaid credit score card bills. These maintain haunting our mind. Once you can see simply indoors your self, you start information that most of the movements were unnecessary. You also can get out of them when you purpose and align them nicely. This is the first-rate manner to come smooth from this vicious cycle of money owed and liabilities.

Victory over Emotions

One of the most important motives for our misery is our feelings. Love, hatred, dislike, and affection are a number of the free-flowing feelings. We join undue importance to topics. The horrible energies and emotions gather and make us sad. Most of these emotions and energies are avoidable. When you appearance deep internal yourself, you find out that maximum of your outbursts have been unreasonable and uncalled for. You may also want to have avoided the terrible energies via the usage of suppressing them. These ultimately cause unhappiness. Your internal moderate will provide you with the know-a way to introspect. This time is completely yours. In this 2d, you're unchallenged. There is not any victory or loss. You are in entire control. There isn't any ego or tussle. You take rational choices. This ends within the beginning of splendid alternatives. You are able to shun awful energies. It is relieving and mild. You end up happy from internal. You get mature and turn out to be affable in real phrases. You should make prudent alternatives closer to strengthening your career and monetary state of affairs. The intuitive strength of the 1/three eye will assist you in assessing your future direction of motion.

You Start Changing from Within

Now, we apprehend that meditation allows you in self-introspection. You recognize the impact of Karma. You moreover understand the impact even the small steps have to need on your existence. You are able to are watching for the outcomes of these movements. This data permits in shaping up a state-of-the-art you.

You emerge as a higher and stepped forward person. Your idea approach starts offevolved offevolved converting from the foundation. Your issues and insecurities vanish slowly and grade by grade. This makes you more confident and sturdy. As your Third eye opens up your physical, emotional and mental properly-being improves. This starts offevolved offevolved reflecting on your common individual. You mellow down. You come to be calm yet confident.

Your route to achievement will become clean. Your desires turn out to be clear and the course vital as heaps as them moreover receives crystal smooth. There isn't always any confusion. The thoughts makes its way through the darkness. It is not any greater simply an entangled form of nerve cells. It receives illuminated.

You begin knowing the strength of your mind. It is a powerhouse. It receives illuminated and you recognize the matters in location. Once the slight comes the direction receives smooth. The undertaking lies in bringing the slight. The pineal gland or the Ajna chakra wishes to be illuminated and activated. This calls for reputation, dedication, and state of affairs. You will need to artwork your manner till here with meditation. You will ought to open your Third eye inwards. This will want staying electricity and resolution. It is a doable assignment. You will sincerely need to commit yourself to it. The direction is not tough. It most effective calls in an effort to hold on foot on it. The adventure is calming and worthwhile. You most effective want to take step one in the direction of it. It will lead you from there.

What is the Pineal Gland?

The pineal gland has remained an enigma and been the hassle of controversy for a long time. In ancient times, it was regarded as "a thriller gland," and theories abounded about its mystical powers. For this motive, it have end up from time to time referred to as "the pineal eye."

The pineal gland is a small reddish-grey gland formed like a pine cone, from which its name is derived. It turn out to be first depicted due to the reality the photo of a pine cone by way of the Sumerians. This pine cone image may be seen inside the paintings of many historic cultures, suggesting that it held amazing significance.

The pineal gland is about one-0.33 of an inch lengthy and belongs to the endocrine machine (the device of hormone-generating glands important for various physical features). It is positioned in the midbrain; it's miles embedded inside the crevice the various left and right hemispheres.

For a long time, the pineal gland emerge as regarded as an unimportant vestigial organ that emerge as unworthy of in-depth research. Even these days, generation has not completely determined all of its abilities—but what is belief thus far indicates its critical importance within the law of numerous physical talents.

The Function of the Pineal Gland

• Its maximum essential function is the producing of the hormone melatonin.

Melatonin regulates the body's circadian rhythm (sleep-wake cycle).

• Melatonin promotes sexual development in every sexes.

• It induces sleep.

• It connects the nervous system with the endocrine device via manner of changing neural signs into hormone secretion.

• It enables modify immune gadget abilties.

• Melatonin regulates the mood and enables us adapt to change. It performs an important function in our happiness and contentment.

• It interacts with many specific organs, further to the blood.

• Studies propose that the melatonin secreted with the aid of the pineal gland may additionally affect cardiovascular health and blood stress, however greater studies is wanted.

Chapter 9: About Your Third Eye

Calling it a "1/three eye" can be very misleading! It's no longer a single eye, it's far eyes stacked on pinnacle of every different. When they'll be inside the identical location, that's if you have actual sight.

In order to look collectively together with your 1/3 eye, you want to set off the second one it without a doubt is called your inner eye. The internal eye can help increase your line of sight in a way that you could no longer commonly be able to see with honestly your outer eyesight.

Your 0.33 eye is located at the brain's proper aspect, at the center of the cranium. It's said to be placed for your pineal gland, that is a tiny gland positioned clearly above your pituitary gland.

The zero.33 eye is shape of like a "psycho-religious" eye that acts as a non secular director for our souls. It is likewise related to psychic capabilities and desires. When you start beginning your 1/3 eye, it's said you will have prolonged psychic skills and extra excellent dreams.

The 1/3 eye may be activated by using the usage of virtually anyone. You don't clearly must go through any particular initiation or schooling to spark off your 0.33 eye.

In order to activate the 1/3 eye, you want to clear out the mind and interest on viewing a unmarried factor. By doing this, you will be able to accentuate the spiritual sensation you get from searching at that factor. Once you've intensified the sensation, place your interest on what is sort of like a flame or spark that is at the component wherein your 1/three eye vision is coming from.

By doing this, you could start to get a imaginative and prescient or photograph this is despatched for your reputation from the zero.33 eye.

Some humans describe seeing top notch colours and a few people say they see pictures.

If you preserve your focus on that image, it will develop in intensity and become an increasing number of smooth. The same is right for the pics that you can see out of your internal thoughts.

It's said that whilst you word collectively in conjunction with your 1/three eye, the whole of truth changes and everything will become a good deal clearer. You are able to divine matters earlier than they appear or are searching in advance to the destiny. It's additionally said that with the resource of taking off your 1/three eye, you may acquire direct notion with precise dimensions of introduction.

The 0.33 eye, or internal eye, is the gate that results within the 4 higher worlds of Yetzirah, Beriah, Yezirah and Asiyah. The sefirot of this global are Keter and Chokmah (the "crown" and the "understanding") on the left, Da'at at the right and Binah (records) at the lowest. It is through these sefirot that one passes from a country of darkness to moderate."

A fuller know-how of this approach can be received via reading the ebook, "Man and His Symbols" via the use of using Carl Jung, who discusses this idea at a few period in Chapter VI.

Jung indicates that via searching on the moon, one is activating the zero.33 eye..."

"The quabbalistic idea of the attention in all its paperwork is an essential key to a deeper information of the world, and to real spiritualization of life on Earth. Once we start to soak up more of this significant variety code, we apprehend that there can be a far more that means to our lives than we had formerly realised. This can best be finished by way of way of way of first starting up up our zero.33 eye. People with open 1/three eyes are more in contact with the arena spherical them, and are capable of push through regular lifestyles pressure to a higher diploma of hobby."

"In this manner it's miles stated that while you learn how to use your zero.33 eye, you are bringing balance into your whole soul and body. While it's clean to understand how this may be finished together with your physical frame, it's a bit more tough to recognize the manner it really works with the religious a part of your being. You see, your bodily body and your spiritual frame are related. So even as you try to supply balance to as a minimum one, you're moreover looking for to do it for the alternative."

"So if you're learning the manner to open up your 0.33 eye, you then definately ought to anticipate that it's going to have some sort of effect for your whole being. One difficulty that would rise up is that you will become more psychic. You may additionally moreover begin to build up messages from the religious realm and sense subjects in advance than they stand up.

Chapter 10: The Fundamentals Truths

There is an eye within the center of the brow that is related to a bodily organ.

The 1/three eye is a supernatural and mysterious organ.

The 1/3 eye gives someone the potential to appearance right into a extraordinary period referred to as 'auras'.

Auras are composed of debris, moderate, and sound waves.

Auras permit one to see topics via clairvoyance or more sensory notion.

Gaining information from all realms of lifestyles can be finished with help from activating your 1/3 eye.

The 1/3 eye is the attention of statistics.

The 0.33 eye is a powerful device that has been overlooked and not noted for decades.

Another purpose behind the 0.33 eye is a country of focus or degree of belief and hobby that refers to better perception to be had to human beings through instinct and insight.

It develops on its non-public as a little one grows and can be expert to an amount.

The 1/3 eye will become activated at the same time as in touch collectively together with your better self which allows you to have get proper of access to to expertise from unique geographical regions of life.

Activating the 1/3 eye can be completed through a clean and focused thoughts similarly to using your imagination.

Activating the 0.33 eye is a totally powerful enjoy that lets in one to turn out to be greater aware about their environment and to have access to data from all geographical areas of reality.

Using your imagination can help cause this u . S ..

When an person has their zero.33 eye activated, they are much more likely to make correct choices that certainly guide an character's life dreams.

The 1/3 eye may be each an asset and a trouble to an man or woman's existence dreams.

Take time to make your self acquainted together in conjunction with your 0.33 eye earlier than trying to prompt it.

This will assist you understand the mechanics behind activating your zero.33 eye similarly to what it looks as if whilst activated.

The zero.33 eye may be very powerful and want to never be used for selfish skills or in reckless techniques.

Using it for selfish features or in reckless strategies can result in awful results.

Third eye activation may be accomplished with 1,000,000 thoughts and photographs that without delay input the thoughts.

When the 0.33 eye is activated, it lets in an individual to have access to know-how from amazing realms of truth.

These are souls of deceased parents which might be anticipating you to call them thru name and use their understanding on your existence dreams.

The 1/3 eye is taken into consideration to be a few issue natural, now not supernatural due to the fact it's miles located within the thoughts.

The 0.33 eye is a effective device that lets in one to peer subjects from one-of-a-kind views and to benefit understanding from all geographical areas of truth.

There are four number one procedures you may spark off their third eye:

One can use cosmic sounds that lets in you to set off their 0.33 eye which includes voice, music, or noises.

Chapter 11: The Key Characteristics Of Third Eye

The 1/three eye is an organ decided in human and super primates that lies simply above the front of the nasal hollow space. It seems as a unmarried, small white dot because it lacks shade pigmentation. In human beings, this is located amongst your eyebrows. For most animals, the 1/three eye's characteristic is to modify bodily temperature and help provoke circadian rhythms; in others, in conjunction with snakes and some amphibians, it permits them discover food or prey via manner of way of sensing movement or changes in mild or humidity.

Other capabilities of the 0.33 eye are merely metaphysical and symbolic in nature. In Indian, Tibetan and Chinese traditions, the 1/3 eye is referred to as ajna chakra or forehead chakra. Its association with telepathy comes from the concept that it stimulates belief beyond regular sight. It also is related to "mind's eye," as well as precognition, clairvoyance, and extrasensory notion of diverse types.

The 0.33 eye is a spiritual and once in a while psychic centre that is idea to be located many of the 2 bodily eyes. Psychics, healers and special masters use this strength to transcend location and time, having access to the arena of higher attention. It also can be a figurative expression for gaining notion or greater notion.

The power of the 1/three eye is idea to be universally possessed through all people. Psychics and other human beings of better popularity have the functionality to use this electricity to get admission to and recognize topics they can't see in regular life. It is thought that this functionality permits humans to go beyond location and time, starting off the mind or soul to higher requirements or geographical regions.

Some ancient people together with the Egyptians believed that a 3rd eye existed in the lower returned of their heads, facing upwards. This is in which the thoughts resided, in the lower back of the eyes. It emerge as furthermore believed that the 1/3 eye became placed in which the student of the attention met each different.

In Hinduism, this non secular strength is called "nāḍī rūpa", which may be translated as "cosmic mild". The Kabbalah moreover refers to this non secular strength as "nefesh ha-kuf", which may be translated as "the soul's mystery".

The zero.33 eye is thought to be a centre of psychic power. This eye is what permits us to accept as true with our instincts, our hunches and belief just so we will apprehend better ideas. When this energy is opened, it produces a psychic awakening or "enlightenment". In order to set off the third eye, humans are taught via using their teachers or masters a manner to assist their minds so you can open this centre. Astral projection and lucid dreaming are common ways of starting off or strengthening the 1/three eye.

The third eye is believed to be the centre of higher recognition. It is idea that once a person dies, the soul passes into the 1/three eye and may live on forever. This might also additionally even allow for a route for souls to enter our realm of life so as for them to maintain their non secular adventure.

Opening this centre of religious strength is regularly taken into consideration a "rebirth". These humans are said to have reached a brand new diploma of know-how and are able to get right of access to better geographical regions of existence. It is stated to offer them the functionality to guide others thru their very private psychic awakening.

It is concept that during order for someone on the way to open or beef up the 1/three eye, they want to learn how to increase their awareness and remember their instincts. The workout of lucid dreaming often allows a person to attention more on being aware in the path of their day, which lets in them extra get right of access to to the power of this centre.

Chapter 12: How To Open The Third Eye

What is 1/3 eye activation

Third Eye is referred to as the pineal gland internal one's mind. The pineal gland produces and regulates melatonin, it's the hormone accountable for our sleep/wake cycles and the way we cope with outdoor stressors. Philosopher Descartes has defined the pineal gland as "the essential seat of the soul". The pituitary gland is also crucial to Third Eye awakening and the 6th chakra in favored, as it's miles chargeable for more than one specific hormone glands in the frame. The pituitary gland, in biology, is often known as the "hold close gland".

When the Third Eye chakra is absolutely balanced or has been activated, each of your mind's hemispheres are capable of feature with whole synchrony. The Third Eye is on occasion known as our body's spiritual middle, and works diligently to interrupt down thoughts that have been delivered on through phantasm, energy, and worry; that allows you to open the thoughts to promote religious healing. The

Third Eye differentiates what we consider to be real with what we apprehend to be actual (or what truly is real). This chakra homes your mental abilities further to intellectual abilities and determines how we examine positive situations, attitudes, and beliefs.

The Third Eye is prepared not most effective the idea of seeing but extra deeply than that the concept of really information what's. This chakra is the deliver of our sense of ethics, morality, and justice (the Third Eye has additionally been said to be the part of us that receives messages from spiritual guides). Psychological competencies associated with the Third Eye (or the pineal gland) are those of instinct and creativeness.

There are severa advantages to awakening your 6th chakra, or Third Eye, and under we've got listed 4 approaches so that you can open your Third Eye followed thru five signs and symptoms and signs that your Third Eye is beginning.

How to Open the Third Eye?

1Touch- Using your index finger, lightly contact the place of your brow located at once among your eyebrows. Rub this small spot in sluggish circles as you breathe deeply (inhaling and exhaling slowly), and believe the chakra starting.

2Essential Oils: Using important oils is a wonderful way to lighten up whilst jogging to rouse your Third Eye. Essential oils may be used to sell stylish health at the equal time as you are drowsing or meditating to balance your chakras. Using an oil diffuser, diffuse numerous drops of sandalwood, chamomile, or myrrh so that it will promote the awakening of your Third Eye.

threeBreathe: This approach can be used constantly at a few level within the day to sell the hole of your Third Eye. Many humans exercise the lousy addiction of shallow respiration without even figuring out. In order to effectively awaken your 6th chakra, it's miles vital which you reputation on and regularly workout deep respiratory. When breathing in, make sure that you're respiratory deep sufficient that your stomach expands with each breathe.

4Clairvoyance Meditation: To exercise this approach, locate a comfortable spot to sit down down and loosen up your frame truly. Once comfortable in a sitting feature, exercising the deep breathing said above for severa mins. Next, visualize the #1 inside the center of your head amongst your eyebrows (at the identical time as nevertheless using the deep respiration sports). Once you have got in reality visualized the number one, pass as an lousy lot due to the fact the extensive variety 2, and repeat this exercising as tons because the big range 10. This meditation exercise will assist workout no longer amazing rest and respiration strategies however also can help to exercise truely visualizing unique shapes and symbols.

Five Signs the Third Eye is Open:

Once you start regularly exercise your intellectual electricity to attempt to open the Third Eye, you'll be conscious fine modifications in the way you see or apprehend matters. Below are five signs and symptoms and signs and signs or symptoms and signs that you may study and regularly act as a signal which you have become a success in awakening your Third Eye:

1You may additionally moreover experience a moderate pressure or spread of warmth among your eyebrows whilst encouraging your Third Eye to open.

2You can also furthermore word an accelerated feeling of intuition, or a stronger "feeling" approximately what's proper to do on the same time as you are confronted with making a decision.

threeAs you inspire your Third Eye to evoke, you could start to word a moderate sensitivity to vibrant mild.

4You can also sense a non-prevent feeling of change inner yourself (frame and thoughts).

5As your Third Eye starts offevolved to open or awaken, you could enjoy moderate headaches, although those normally get up much less and masses much less regularly as you hold exercising starting your Third Eye.

Symptoms and factor-outcomes

After setting up your 1/three eye, you are going to experience some numerous matters with the purpose to tell you whether or not or no longer your organising meditation have come to be a success. Now, thinking about the reality that every person is superb, we might not enjoy the identical matters or to the same make bigger. Some need to have very diffused signs and signs and signs, at the same time as others can also have a few very overwhelming consequences. However, regardless of how intensely you experience the ones signs, there appear like some signs maximum human beings enjoy.

Short Term Symptoms and Side Effects

Here are a number of the symptoms and signs and symptoms and signs and symptoms and signs you could assume right after organising your 0.33 eye, and so that you can depart after more than one days or possibly weeks.

Pressure on Forehead: A stress on the brow is for lots the first actual symptom they get and is a few issue maximum people enjoy during, or proper after completing the zero.33 eye beginning meditation. The strain can become pretty excessive while you meditate or think about your 1/three eye, as it's far an awful lot more sensitive now

Tingling Sensation: A tingling sensation on the forehead or crown chakra is likewise one of the first actual symptoms and symptoms you can anticipate even as you open your 1/3 eye. It might be a ordinary itchy or humming feeling in your forehead that doesn't leave when you scratch it.

Headache: In addition to the feeling of strain in your head, you could additionally enjoy complications. So take the time to relaxation and permit the headache to move away.

Crackling or Popping Sound: Some human beings say they pay interest a crackling or loud popping sound inner their head after putting in the 0.33 eye. This is the activation of the pineal gland, that is positioned inside the center of the mind, which is also wherein the sound has a tendency to originate from.

Seeing Lights While Meditating: Many humans see lighting while meditating once they have opened the 0.33 eye. This is often in sorts of string or spiral original lighting in inexperienced, red or white (even though can be any color).

Seeing Images While Meditation: Many human beings experience seeing pics, frequently instances a watch shaped item, at the same time as meditating.

Emotional Imbalance: Opening the 1/three eye may additionally have a few normal effects on human beings's feelings and some revel in temper swings and episodes of disappointment wherein they sense like crying for no right cause.

Nightmares: An open 1/3 eye can offer nightmares more regularly within the starting, which should leave after multiple days or maybe weeks. You might also observe that your goals grow to be lots extra vibrant and which you consider more of your goals.

Long Term Symptoms and Benefits

Improved Visual Awareness: An open third eye can enhance your reputation and eyesight, and make you greater sensitive to impressions round you.

Improved Focus: Your popularity also can boom extensively and also you become a good buy greater centered and clean minded.

Improved Memory: You can also revel in that your attention improves and you've got got a far much less complex time remembering data.

Sensitive to Energies: As a part of the spiritual popularity, you come to be an lousy lot extra touchy to energies round you. This will will let you to your development of psychic skills.

Improved Intuition: setting up the 1/3 eye can also notably decorate your intuition and you've an less difficult time making selections based totally on your intuitive senses and not to your logical and physical senses on my own.

Otherworldly Impressions: One symptom which could frighten many humans is the truth that you could get impressions from beings no longer of this bodily worldwide collectively with spirits or entities.

Ability to Sense the Truth: Many humans enjoy the feeling of knowledge the truth in particular situations and be capable of see subjects greater without a doubt.

Psychic Abilities: Opening the 0.33 eye can extensively advantage you on your approach of growing psychic talents and is some difficulty many people advices nearly about psychic exercising, as you can connect to your spirituality and popular energies.

Third Eye Awakening Checklist

Check the containers beneath to record the unique signs and symptoms and signs and symptoms you've got got were given from your 1/3 eye awakening exercising.

After 1 weekAfter 1 month or more

  Tingling sensation on forehead

 Improved Visual cognizance

  Tingling sensation on Crown Chakra

Improved Intuition

Pressure on Forehead

Improved interest

Crackling or popping sound

Sensing the reality in conditions

Seeing lighting whilst meditating

Otherworldly Impressions

Nightmares or colourful desires

Sensitive to energies

Emotional Imbalance

Improved Focus

Seeing pics at the same time as meditating

Clairvoyant impressions

Chapter 13: How To Awake The Third Eye

Opening your 1/3 eye takes time and exercising. While you could have an enjoy, together with in the route of meditation, in that you enjoy a large rush of awakening, it'll no longer be virtually woke up via one enjoy. Rather, the awakening is a way and also you need to take it sluggish and decide to it if you are going to enjoy a complete awakening.

Beginning with meditation is a super way to begin starting off your 1/three eye, but there are extra tactics that you may open it as properly. Some of these are practices that you ought to set apart time for, while others are ones that you may use for your normal each day existence. As you're the use of these practices, it's far critical to apprehend that your zero.33 eye awakening is probably a very spiritual and character machine, however having it in an awakened u . S . Way that you are going to mix it into your each day existence. Awakening your 1/3 eye need to now not eat all your time and result in you doing no longer a few thing but focusing at the awoke u . S . A . Of your 0.33 eye. Rather, you need to set aside some time however otherwise attention on important your existence as you generally could. As your third eye awakens, you may phrase versions about yourself that stem from this awakening machine. However, you ought to preserve essential your each day existence and permitting these modifications to definitely integrate, in choice to driving them. Anything pressured isn't herbal, and consequently may additionally moreover inhibit the outlet device in your 1/3 eye.

Learn to Silence Your Mind

In addition to proper meditation, exercising silencing your thoughts. When we skip about our every day lives, there has an inclination to be pretty a few chatter and noise in our minds which can maintain us constantly distracted and focused on the whole lot except what we are doing. A terrific manner to help your 1/3 eye awakening is to discover ways to silence your thoughts and recognition most effective at the undertaking handy. When you do, your thoughts is probably targeted, and the history may be silenced. It is commonly inner' those silences that the 0.33 eye and our psychic talents will kick in and take region.

While it isn't viable to completely forestall wondering, you should stay very intentional collectively together with your questioning manner and attention particularly on what you want to be thinking about relying on what you're physical doing. The 0.33 eye chakra has an inclination to "activate" and art work in the course of the "in amongst" times that take area amongst thoughts and reviews. Therefore, in case you need to intentionally prompt it, you want to intentionally set apart area for those in-among moments to reveal up. When you do, make certain that you are paying interest and are aware of when they display up so you can attention on them and workout strengthening your functionality to set off them on every occasion you desire.

Practice Tuning In

If contemporary society has taught us a few issue, it's that we should overlook approximately approximately the little voice inner and do what's "right" based totally on what others have knowledgeable us to recall is proper. We are frequently lead off target from our instinct, and therefore we warfare to actually be aware of it. If you'll don't forget, your intuition is your 0.33 eye speaking to you. If you want to rouse your 1/3 eye and assist it open similarly, you need to reputation on putting off the selection to disregard this voice and in fact music into it.

When you experience or pay attention a few aspect popping out of your intuition, take the time to well known it, and then surely be aware of it. Do some element it says, after which examine what occurs as a stop quit end result. In normally lifestyles will become less difficult, a threat is averted, we apprehend or observe some element we may additionally moreover

moreover have omitted, or matters are otherwise "higher" conventional. Sometimes the ones realizations won't be as apparent, however they do exist. Learning to song into your instinct manner you are studying to renowned and supply credit score score on your 1/three eye. And, because the announcing says "wherein your hobby goes, energy flows" this means that that during case you're intentionally being attentive to your 1/3 eye and your intuition, it's going to keep talking to you. The more you song in and pay interest, the higher your "relationship" or connection is probably, and the higher effects you will get from tuning in.

Explore Your Natural Creativity

Our innovative aspects are in massive component linked to our third eye. Those who are surprisingly current will be predisposed to be very current, or interested in developing their progressive competencies. If you need to attach closer to your zero.33 eye, practice embracing your creativity and letting it free. Even in case you don't suppose you're an amazing artist or you're inexperienced with diverse art work forms, workout them besides. Let your imagination take over and create some thing that entails thoughts. Don't preserve expectancies of what it must or shouldn't appear to be, without a doubt create. You will find out that while you do that, your 0.33 eye chakra will enjoy more higher honestly. Remember, your 1/three eye is also your "thoughts's eye" which means that that it's far your imagination. When you create from your imagination, you are straight away growing out of your 1/three eye. It can be an outstanding enjoy along your awakening way.

Take Time to Ground Yourself

Your 1/three eye can take you into the non secular realm thru your thoughts's eye and your intuition, and on the same time as you are not cautious it could have an effect on your capability to stay grounded. When you are running together together with your zero.33 eye, you have to be simultaneously running in conjunction with your root chakra and grounding yourself. You can do that by meditating for your root chakra and bear in mind real etheric roots connecting you to the center of the Earth. This is a exceptional manner to counterbalance your 0.33 eye and preserve you rooted whilst also permitting you to discover your awakening.

When you don't make an effort to root your self, you could enjoy what's referred to as "overstimulation", because of this that that your 1/3 eye is operating extra than your one of a kind chakras. This can reason strain, soreness, being beaten, and lots of different undesirable reviews. When the approach of awakening becomes uncomfortable, humans are much more likely to keep away from it and consequently they may be able to locate themselves now not seeking to similarly their awakening. Furthermore, they'll near their eye out of fear and have hassle looking to pass back to the awakening system at any detail within the destiny. To keep away from being overwhelmed and the discomfort, ensure you're continuously focusing on grounding your self. If you are not a top fan of meditation, you could moreover allow your naked feet to connect without delay to the Earth, as this is a notable physical grounding technique.

Exercise Your Third Eye

Exercising your 0.33 eye is a amazing manner to help guide its starting. It additionally will growth your power and abilties, which means you could have an much less tough time preserving it open, the usage of it on a ordinary foundation, and activating your psychic talents at any time that you preference. The following are outstanding wearing activities you may exercise to help you help your third eye setting up.

One brilliant way is to do meditations that incorporate all of the chakras. Similar to how it is vital to ground and cognizance for your root chakra, you have to additionally popularity on strengthening your distinct chakras, too. While you may desire to frequently cognizance on strengthening and developing your skills with them one after the other, it's miles crucial which you keep to present reputation to each of them. A brilliant meditation is to region down and meditate, then accept as true with your chakras separately. Start together with your root chakra and work your manner up for your crown chakra. As you skip, agree with each one shining brighter and brighter till it's miles shining its brightest. You also can recollect them spinning clockwise, as they may be a fluid power that moves, they do not genuinely beam like a lamp, but as an possibility swirl like a whirlpool.

Another extremely good way to paintings along facet your 0.33 eye is to do dream art work. Using lucid dreaming meditations, and running within the route of dream interpretation are each great techniques to exercise dream work. Lucid dreaming is usually completed the use of meditations, in that you allow yourself to go into a dream state and then you definitely mentally control your self inside the dream america of the united states. It allows you to be on top of factors of your dream, in preference in your dream be in control like they commonly are. Dream interpretation itself calls with a purpose to allow the dream to flow manifestly, and then you interpret it upon waking up. The first-rate way to do this is to put in writing approximately your dream in the moments after you've got have been given woken up. You can then interpret them in your very personal, or buy a dream interpretation magazine to help you interpret specific elements interior' the dream.

Allowing your imagination to flow manifestly and on its personal is some different top notch manner to play together along with your 1/3 eye. Practice sitting in a meditative united states, after which allow your imagination go along with the flow. Just test it everywhere it is going. During this sort of meditation, there may be no want to draw your hobby decrease again to any precise location, you could surely allow it go to anywhere it wants to be. You can also allow your creativeness to go together with the drift whilst you're developing along side via drawing, writing, pottery, or special crafts. Allowing your meditation to take fee and faithfully following it let you feel extra related for your 1/three eye, and may help beneficial useful resource its awakening.

Intuition lead breaks are every other fantastic manner to bolster your 1/3 eye. Like with gambling together with your creativeness, you are letting your intuition lead the way. This manner which you skip anywhere and carry out a little aspect that your intuition is telling you to. So, in case your intuition tells you to head sit down thru a particular tree in a exquisite park and appearance in a certain direction, you do it. When you comply with your instinct this way, you leave your self open to receiving mental "downloads" which may be often full of records that can be beneficial to your present state. You may want to in all likelihood studies something about yourself, be guided to take a particular movement in a positive state of affairs, or in any other case revel in cause carry out a touch aspect. All of those stem from your 1/three eye steering and want to be commemorated while you experience them in the route of this time. If you may recollect, honoring your instinct is a first rate manner to set off and increase the strength of your 1/three eye.

The very last remarkable way to workout your 0.33 eye is to bolster your psychic skills.

Whenever you experience one of the clairs, allow your self to in fact embody it. If it's miles displaying you some factor or encouraging you to do some component or be given as genuine with a excessive first-class piece of records with out a logical clarification, do your nice to take a look at it. When you do, you will be strengthening the capability and your connection in your 1/3 eye.

Opening your 1/3 eye is a manner. There is the device of commencing it for the number one time, after which the approach of keeping it open. When you nurture your 0.33 eye, you will discover that existence is wonderful and plenty less complicated than you may have ever believed it may be. Our zero.33 eye can be taken into consideration our very very very own covered "northern big name" guiding us within the course we want to move. When we comply with it and we pay attention to what it has to say, we're virtually guided to wherein we need to be as a way to have the incredible reviews.

You have in all likelihood had commonly wherein you located your zero.33 eye's guidance without knowledge it because of the reality your 1/three eye speaks to you through your intuition. When you open it deliberately, but, it will become simpler to comply with and explore deliberately, and not move in a first-rate course because of any fear you could have of paying attention to your internal voice. When you aren't intentionally being attentive to it and are ignorant of the electricity of your 1/three eye, it can be easy to be led off target after which come to be feeling responsible or out of vicinity because of the fact you probably did some issue you probably did now not want to or that modified into no longer properly for you no matter some component inner you telling you that you need to have in no way finished it within the first place.

When you're putting in place your 1/3 eye, make sure which you set aside time to preserve doing it. There may be times in which you don't continuously popularity on it, but regular you need to make investments a few hours regular with week on operating collectively along with your 1/3 eye chakra. This will help make certain that you are staying related with it and that it is serving you inside the most effective manner viable. As a stop result, you can discover that life is a first rate deal greater balanced, nice, appealing, and realistic. You will discover greater that means on your life, and you will locate that it's miles less complicated to comply along with your inner compass with out worry which you are doing the wrong issue. In reality, you can have a much less difficult time being your self, and the judgment and beliefs of others will no longer have this type of strong functionality to impact your very personal beliefs and you may be capable of revel in a splendid deal freer.

Chapter 14: The Advantages Of An Awakened Third Eye

Our two regular eyes we use are essential and the zero.33 eye has extra importance as well. With this eye, you're capable of see beyond ordinary imaginative and prescient into belongings you in no way knew existed. To a few people, it's miles nonsense and evil at the identical time as some agree with it is a means closer to a better level of intelligence and interest. Some religions consider it's miles the gateway to connect with God. Some maintain in mind it as a route to beautify interest and knowledge of the area spherical them. You need to awaken the 1/three eye to have a deeper data of yourself and life. Using the zero.33 eye could make a international of distinction to everybody due to the reality:

You are capable of see past the physical seen thru a normal eyesight

You are able to stimulate the 6th sense

You are able to take a look at other unique energies like non-physical beings and auras which is probably round you

You are capable of revel in folks that aren't inside the same feature as you are

You become greater open to 3 various things

You may have a clean expertise of your beyond

You may additionally have a intellectual intuition to installation what has been troubling your peace of thoughts

You ought to have a wonderful angle on life

You ought to have extra progressed and great competencies and competencies

You ought to have an out-of-frame experience

You will own an advanced intuition

You will start to recognize matters deeply

Your ideals could be greater established.

You are in full manage of your reaction to traumatic situations.

Your connection for your spirit guides and the universe can be better.

Your hearing sensitivity to otherworldly voices and sounds will increase

Your intelligence and thinking ability can be advanced.

You is probably able to be in charge of your thoughts and movements

Your belief of problems and lifestyles, in preferred, will trade.

Your life turns into greater massive and peaceful.

When awakening your 1/three eye, you have to undertaking your self with the questions of what and why? Why are you awakening the attention which you aren't in a function to appearance? What are the advantages obtained from the meditation? What will you benefit even as you open the 1/3 eye? Understanding the way of doing so will offer a platform to make you understand the results of your movements. Your deeper records will help you decide the right quantity of power to commit to the attainment of the purpose. You can be in a extraordinary function what's to be finished on a hit final touch. Realizing that the 1/3 eye gives you the psychic capability that lets in you to look beings from the religious geographical regions, the query is -- for what purpose on Earth would possibly you need to collect some aspect like that? There are sincerely plenty of benefits that include beginning your psychic eye. The maximum vital advantage is that you may get a whole new aircraft of information, balance, and a more top notch of existence. Explained underneath are the advantages of setting up the 0.33 eye:

Kick Bad Habits

It has been a human behaviour to be short sighted in life. Planning earlier is a problem to many which bring about lousy behavior. They take to 3 behavior like smoking and eating appeared as if it'd deliver rest even though brief-lived. With an open 1/three eye, you are able to choose out out this brief-sightedness and addictions in a special moderate and as a end result capable of eliminate them from your existence.

Better Relationships

Relationships may be impacted through someone's short. Most relationships start on a happy and ideal word but come to be in fights. They change heated feelings and they permit the combat to rip them aside. But if human beings have their 1/3 eye open on this sort of relationship, they may be able to visualize the issues in a superb way. You can be able to see your shortcomings and be capable of exchange the situation for the better and improve the connection together with your companion, own family or buddies.

Accept Yourself

There comes a time in your existence when you experience dejected, by myself, much less lucky or worthless. Do what? You are nevertheless important and precise. In this example, the 1/three eye may be of awesome help to make you have a better know-how of your life's purpose. You gained't revel in dejected. You also can have religious courses to self-stability.

Reach Your Goals

People do set dreams they reason to gather interior a given span of time. The dreams can be difficult until you experience no motivation to warfare on. You sense you do not private what it takes or the constraints can be many. With an opened zero.33 eye, your thoughts may be set on accomplishing the desires due to the truth you'll be decided. You will view the goals truely and they'll seem very smooth.

Be Happy

People strive for matters they apprehend a good way to cause them to happy but come to be not achieving the goal. With the 1/3 eye open, you'll revel in more content and also you obtained't interest on petty situations that waste it slow. Doing so will ultimately make you experience satisfied.

Become More Spiritual

People depend extra on generation thereby losing the close to connection with one's self. The soul desires to be valued and nourished. The 1/3 eye lets in you to personal non secular boom and connects your soul with the universe.

Chapter 15: About Third Eye Healing

Is it real? Is it hype? Is there clinical proof to help the claim that tapping gently on 'your 0.33 eye' can heal pretty an awful lot some thing?

The brief solution is that the jury remains out. There are many documented instances of humans who have expert healing benefits after receiving treatment, but now not sufficient to prove that this recovery electricity is reliable.

Instead, the bulk of research factors to our body's capability to use mild for recovery via phototherapy. This approach using your eyes or exclusive tools to polish mild on precise areas of the body with the intention to impact excessive first-rate alternate.

When you visit your doctor and that they use a laser or different moderate remedy as a part of their remedy, they are gambling into the theories of phototherapy, which has been round for hundreds of years. This historical Chinese artwork is referred to as Qi Gong and includes meditation, postures and visualization to result in healing through moderate.

The idea of slight treatment as a way to heal the frame is not new. At least one check shows that Egyptian medical medical doctors used a way referred to as "ablution with sun energy" over 3000 years inside the beyond.

While we might not understand precisely the way it works, there may be some evidence that shows that the use of mild need to have a powerful impact on our physical and emotional fitness.

Research has set up that treatment via slight can enhance blood movement and metabolism, which improves health in latest.

In particular, some research recommend that phototherapy may be useful for patients who be concerned thru a scenario referred to as SAD (seasonal affective disorder). This state of affairs is characterised through despair and fatigue at a few stage in the wintry weather months even as the times are shorter. While there is despite the fact that not a whole lot of research in this factor of phototherapy, there can be a few proof to signify that it could assist people with SAD get a better night time time's sleep.

While there is not sufficient studies to show that light remedy is the crucial component to splendid health, we do realise that moderate does have blessings for our fitness.

There are many fantastic sorts of light remedy that could assist deal with a massive style of ailments from depression and ache to fantastic styles of cancer. For example, photodynamic remedy entails the usage of a photosensitive drug that may be implemented topically or through manner of way of injection. This treatment lighting up effective tissue and destroys it in response to a particular sort of bacterial contamination, consequently blockading the increase of greater bacteria.

Additionally, laser remedy uses laser slight to break up pus, kill micro organism or purpose special varieties of tissue harm.

Therapeutic facial manipulation is a few different manner of the use of light to have an impact on our health. Used with the useful

useful resource of massage therapists and others who deal with their sufferers, this remedy usually includes arms which might be manipulated at the same time as they may be blanketed with a blanket or a material. The blanket reflects the affected person's very own herbal slight to assist stimulate recovery, even though it is unknown precisely how this idea works.

Another example of the usage of mild for remedy is ear candling. The concept behind this remedy is that lighting fixtures a candle and the use of it to create suction lifts wax, impurities, and other debris out of your ear canal. Many humans swear through ear candling as a manner to relieve ear ache, but there may be no real evidence to another time up those claims.

While there is a lot of controversy surrounding the claim that healing energy might also lie inside us, we do need to preserve an open mind. A present day study advocated that amongst 18 and forty four percentage of ladies who've handed thru cervical maximum cancers screening confirmed a slight change in their Pap smear readings after they acquired phototherapy treatments.

Additionally, some of human beings have said having success the use of mild as treatment to deal with diseases like cancer, arthritis, despair and sleep troubles.

If you need to check with moderate remedy, there are numerous one-of-a-type kinds of mild that can be used in diverse techniques. Some people like to use a unique lamp (known as an "ultraviolet lamp") which emits moderate within the ultraviolet spectrum. This can be especially useful for patients who can also have a compromised immune device or for individuals who want to use it to address maximum cancers or psoriasis. There also are pink, blue and inexperienced lights which can be useful for treating positive pores and skin conditions.

Chapter 16: The Steps To Heal Your Third Eye

There are many approaches to connect with the non secular international and your intuition. In fact, the ones techniques were spherical for heaps of years. But did you recognize that you can additionally heal your 0.33 eye thru the usage of this non secular method?

The 1/3 eye is the gap among your eyes and forehead which represents our connection to better frequencies of power. It's wherein we gather visions, mind that come from deep inner, innovative idea, or synchronicities about our life path.

Why is the 0.33 eye the most effective power middle in our body? Because it connects us to our middle, that is the spiritual essence of who we are. The bodily frame and thoughts have a restrained "range" or "attain" for energy. But our spirit can bypass past all boundaries, along side time, vicinity or maybe lack of existence.

The human spirit will have many capabilities that can't be accessed from another part of the frame or mind. It's the relationship to our limitless self and to the author of our existence. We want to use all parts of our better being at the same time as we're alive on this human enjoy, no longer truly one component.

We can heal our 0.33 eye by using the usage of connecting to the spiritual middle of who we are by way of doing some thing that offers remarkable pressure consolation: Yoga, meditation, prayer, visualization or maybe taking an extended stroll in nature.

The zero.33 eye is a totally effective and sacred place of the frame. We are all ambassadors for our spirit, so we want to be in a pleasant and loving kingdom of thoughts whilst connecting to it.

How can we heal our 1/three eye? It's done through sending love and gratitude as a good deal because the divine part of ourselves:

First, we grow to be aware that there can be a part of us that exists beyond time, space and dying. It's the spiritual essence all of us percentage: countless life, countless love and endless possibilities.

Next, we're able to send the message of affection and gratitude to our non secular center. We can do it with the aid of meditating, writing down our thoughts, announcing a prayer or perhaps surely sitting quietly.

Finally, we come to be aware that we are a completely unique spirit proper right here inside the worldwide and that the divine part of our better self is proper right here with us constantly and everywhere. We revel in the power inside this dating of duality: spirit brings cognizance and attention brings popularity of who we are at a religious degree.

We do now not need to adventure everywhere in area or time to do those gadgets. We can do those practices truly by way of the usage of being privy to them. That's the superb detail approximately meditation and prayer: they may be within us, now not above us. We have the spiritual electricity inner us that could heal our 1/3 eye any time we need through the use of our conscious mind or perhaps our intuitive thoughts as steerage.

170

Here are some steps on the way to heal your 1/3 eye:

1. Become privy to the 1/three eye, this is proper amongst your eyes and brow. It's included by way of way of a veil that you need to put off. That veil is our cognizance on cloth mind and illusions, which prevent us from connecting to our spiritual middle.

2. Become conscious that there may be a better spiritual a part of yourself that might manual you in lifestyles. This better religious self has all understanding that you want to achieve your complete functionality, take place your goals and heal both emotionally and physical.

three. Become conscious that your religious middle is growing your complete life revel in. It will hold growing until you balance your mind and feelings, understand the horrific mind and feelings which might be getting within the manner of connecting to it, and heal them. All of this takes location robotically at the identical time as our interest is centered at the better self.

4. Be thankful for your better self for the entirety that it has already given you in lifestyles: a body, mind and spirit able to endless consciousness, love and peace.

5. Surrender the part of you that isn't always the religious center: a part of your individual, feelings and thoughts.

6. Ask your spirit's help to connect greater on the aspect of your spiritual middle via asserting it aloud: "My better self is right proper right here with me commonly and anywhere."

7. Allow your self to experience any strong feelings related to connecting to your non secular middle, along side worry or happiness. These emotions appear even as you're doing some element you have got never carried out in advance than, like connecting in your better self. They are there to provide you comments, no longer to prevent you from healing your 1/3 eye.

eight. Understand that your spirit is the deliver of all lifestyles and love and that this love is commonly flowing via you and to the entirety else. Just relax and permit this reference to the spiritual middle of who you're.

9. Relax your frame and thoughts. Let skip of all pressure. You can do it by means of the use of taking an prolonged stroll in nature or perhaps a slow, deep breath if you are experiencing anxiety or blockages to your frame and mind.

10. Receive the affection it's far flowing thru you and in the direction of you even as your 0.33 eye is healed. The more love that enters the frame, the extra recuperation power there may be for every part of you, in conjunction with your 0.33 eye.

* * *

The second truth in the better religious mind is that our souls are not absolutely fashioned until we die and attain the 7th diploma of enlightenment. We are aware about being vain, understanding that we have died but our essence does no longer fade away. In reality, at the fifth stage of enlightenment, we enjoy as despite the fact that we've got have been given already died and are "re-living" this level in lifestyles through a enjoy of déjà vu. Thus, if at any time an individual is careworn or afraid they will die into their soul or spirit focus and locate that they may be even though alive and breathing. The first is that we are able to die and the second is that our souls or spirit bodies will preserve to stay after physical loss of life.

Chapter 17: And If Your Third Eye Is Blocked?

There's a reason why humans say "he/she has eyes, and one in the decrease lower back in their head." Our three-eyed pal is placed within the center of our brow! The 1/3 eye chakra, moreover known as Ajna, lets in us to peer thru illusions and matters that aren't what they seem.

The 0.33 eye is frequently termed the "6th experience," because it permits us to peer into or apprehend matters that cannot be seen with our bodily eyes.

Through our zero.33 eye, we are able to gain records about ourselves and the arena spherical us. Adepts take delivery of as real with that this chakra offers us perception and intuition. Read directly to look a manner to open your 1/3 eye chakra...

What is the Third Eye Chakra?

The 0.33 eye chakra is located in among our brows. It is every now and then known as the "thoughts's eye," as it gives us psychic talents.

The 1/three eye chakra additionally helps us with visualization, imagination, and creativity.

The 0.33 eye chakra is activated through meditation, prayer and silent contemplation. In order for your 1/three eye to open, you want to be focused on a incredible purpose. That effective purpose allow you to set yourself aside from the ones spherical you.

Your zero.33 eye from time to time has a unique color from your brow strains and crown. This way that it's far greater open or energetic than others inside the region. Opening your 0.33 eye approach which you in the period in-between are able to use this psychic capability to your advantage instead of letting it have an impact on others negatively.

This is a question you'll in all likelihood have been asking yourself lately, if you've been having problem seeing matters as they really are.

In this put up, we're going to talk approximately what need to motive those "1/3 eye blocks" and the manner to smooth them up! We'll also speak approximately a way to change your manner of lifestyles conduct just so the ones blocks don't show up anymore.

Why do your 1/3 eye blocks take location?

There are many reasons why you may be experiencing 1/3 eye blocks. Some of the most not unusual motives are:

Physical or emotional trauma. When you revel in a trauma, your hobby contracts, and may sometimes block off your 0.33 eye. Physical stress. Mental strain or fatigue. If you're tired or confused, in particular if you don't address your thoughts thru meditating, you can block off your 1/3 eye. Eating risky substances. Processed or sugary elements could make it extra tough that lets in you to awareness and clean your head. Unhealthy way of life conduct. Drinking alcohol can purpose blurry imaginative and prescient and cloudy questioning, which blocks off the 0.33 eye. Being egotistical.

If so I clearly have the therapy!

Meditation is an paintings that genuinely everyone can do. It has many benefits which consist of decreasing stress, being greater privy to your emotions, or maybe having physical health advantages.

It's critical to now not have distractions while meditating - try not to watch TV or use your laptop so you are free from all the outside noise and seen stimuli.

To begin with I suggest a guided meditation. You are guided through this meditation to attain your medial "eye" via paying attention to the person at the recording and following along. Another exceptional manner to do it's far in whole silence. Just sit down and do now not a few aspect for 15 minutes. It is tough at the start however after some practice you may learn how to clean your mind and discover peace indoors yourself.

Once you find this peace interior yourself you'll have greater notable interactions with different human beings. In turn others should have a effective feeling about you and can be much more likely to open up and emerge as pals with you. It has been showed that meditation brings people together and makes them more likely to love each certainly one of a kind. Thus important to a great stronger friendship.

If you have ever been bothered with the resource of the usage of a physical or emotional blockage, you've got possibly moreover professional religious blockages. An clean technique to this problem is probably find out new procedures of bearing on and experiencing existence. If a spiritual setting up is right in advance than you, but, it might be useful to recognise what a blockage looks as if. You can also see how your very personal blockages appear in others.

Spiritual blockages show up in precise methods. There are instances whilst humans are open and take on new testimonies or conditions, but they come to be blocked after they face a frustrating or uncomfortable state of affairs. Some of those situations encompass: managing different people, or even one's very own emotions; having to confront uncomfortable situations, which include developing a hard preference; or coming across new elements of oneself. Each of these reviews can be tough to deal with.

Introverts are people who are often blocked thru environmental conditions, but similarly they've got their non-public blocks that come from within themselves. Introverts revel in physical and intellectual blockages that make the ones situations more tough for them than for extroverts.

Chapter 18: The Crystal Healing

Utilize restoration stones which have the vibrational Chakra and frequency color due to the fact the 0.33 eye chakra repair electricity float and to smooth away. Stones, crystals, and gemstones that speak the same color, energy possessions, and intellectual affinities can assist to balance this power middle. For instance, pink jasper, amethyst, and ruby can help to alleviate the strain of Rajasic goals inside the Heart Chakra.

Green tourmaline or any natural tea can be used for the Heart Chakra. You also can use a quartz crystal or look up statistics approximately it on the internet. Another beneficial stone is black obsidian, that allows you to help dispose of indoors highbrow encumbrances on your mind.

If you have got got been worried with self-precipitated Chakra healing, it might be hard to alternate your view of yourself. You need to think which you are more potent than those feelings and emotions. If you need to maintain the Chakra easy and healthful, then you definitely definately want to apply a combination of spiritual healing and emotional cleansing practices.

If someone isn't always aware about the center power they've got or if they're having problem connecting with their internal energy, then they need to discover a way wherein they are able to express their very non-public strengths.

Rejuvenating the Chakras

Chakra cleansings are particularly beneficial. However, you ought to use caution that allows you to keep away from terrible the body. It is brilliant to talk about with a professional. A suitable chakra cleaner will permit you to to connect to your internal self, and it can provide you with beneficial records approximately your emotions so that you can hold yourself wholesome. Over time, the interest of the chakras receives less difficult and much less hard because it will become everyday and less difficult to carry out with exercising.

There are many techniques to do Chakra cleansing. Meditation is the maximum not unusual manner of doing it. It is also important to do each day so that you can maintain your life balance every day.

For maximum human beings, they will be not capable of apprehend their chakra color. Perfect stones on your 1/three eye chakra encompass:

Amethyst: promotes inner and enriches your instinct Spirituality and advantages

Lapis Lazuli: this rock connects you and Draws your interest. Knowledge, know-how, perfection, protection, and expression.

Fluorite: Fluorite invites extraordinary and cleanses your energy on your space. Stability, installation discernment, and consciousness. It lets you apprehend and maintain beliefs.

Shungite: the energy that's released neutralizes in some unspecified time in the future of 0.33 eye chakra restoration, supporting increase a stable region to treatment and speech concealed emotions

Put your eye circles on the grid formation the photo above inside the distance and your forehead. It is probably tons less complicated to place the rocks at the set up order beside you and then pass them in case you do not have absolutely everyone that will help you set the 1/3 eye chakra stones. As speedy as you've got finished the grid, close your eyes and breathe moving into a country.